Praise for the outdoor classic, *No Room for Bears:*

"Having walked Alaskan bear trails with Frank Dufresne, and having crouched beside him in the devil's club while a monster brownie reared up to blot the sky, I can testify that no one knows more about bears, no one else could have written this thrilling and authentic American classic. And no one can read it without getting goosebumps, or finish it without sharing the author's hope that these great beasts will be treated 'with dignity and compassion.' This is a life work by one of the finest outdoor writers of our time...."

——*Corey Ford*

"It is most fortunate that this accurately descriptive volume should appear at this critical time when the future existence of the giant bears on Admiralty is in question. No one is better equipped than Frank Dufresne, either in experience or writing ability, to draw this splendid comparison with conditions of more than 30 years ago. This should prove to be another classic by the former regional director of the U.S. Fish and Wildlife Service in Alaska."

——*C. R. Gutermuth*
Wildlife Management Institute

Other Books by Frank Dufresne

New Edition of an Outdoor Classic

No Room for Bears

A Wilderness Writer's Experiences with a Threatened Breed
Frank Dufresne

Foreword by Roger Caras

With drawings by Rachel S. Horne

Alaska Northwest Books™
Anchorage • Seattle

Dedicated to my wife Klondy, who has looked with me upon many wild Alaska bears and who shares my hope that coming generations of humans will treat these great beasts with dignity and compassion.

No Room for Bears was first published in the United States by Holt, Rinehart and Winston, New York, 1965. The text of the 1991 edition was published by arrangement with Harold Ober Associates, Inc., New York. Drawings by Rachel S. Horne were published by arrangement with Henry Holt and Company, Inc., New York.

Library of Congress Cataloging-in-Publication Data
Dufresne, Frank.
No room for bears: a wilderness writer's experiences with a threatened breed / Frank Dufresne.
p.   cm.
Reprint. Originally published: New York: Holt, Rinehart, and Winston, 1965.
ISBN 0-88240-414-8
1. Bears — Anecdotes.   2. Dufresne, Frank.   I. Title.
QL795.B4D8   1991
599.74'446'09798 — dc20   91-15629
                                                              CIP
Front cover photograph by Tom Walker/AllStock
Design by Ernst Reichl
Cover design by Kate L. Thompson

Alaska Northwest Books™
A division of GTE Discovery Publications, Inc.
22026 20th Avenue S.E.
Bothell, WA 98021
Printed on acid-free recycled paper in the United States of America

¶ Foreword

A lot of men and women have walked in the woods. They have often been people addicted to wild places and able to read the world of wonders around them with practiced eyes. Many of these wilderness wanderers have visited Alaska and some have remained. Some have pressed their palm prints upon the destiny of the land.

Some have told stories we all must learn by heart, lessons of salvation and ecological damnation. They have told them so well that their words have the ring of classical prose. Frank Dufresne was such a man. He went to Alaska and stayed for more than four decades. His observations and concerns were not only printed on paper, they were imprinted on the minds of those of us lucky enough to discover him while he flourished. Rachel Carson wandered by the edge of the sea; Frank Dufresne walked with the bears.

Several have written about bears, some have even created whole books on these magnificent, cranky giants. Bears have been, in their way, bellwethers. Because they are so conspicuous, so imposing, they have led the way into good times and bad. When the wildlife of a region is getting into trouble, chances are the bears, if bears there are, will be among the first to suffer. When an area is being properly protected, the bears will be among the most obvious beneficiaries. Frank Dufresne wrote about bears with such affection, precision, and such depth of concern that his book, *No Room for Bears*, is reckoned a classic of not only the literature of the bear but of nature writing of any description.

He told us what could happen, and many people wondered, "Can he be right?" Some of us knew that he was, and we applauded the fact that a spokesman had risen up from among us and called out to the whole world, "Beware, be warned, you stand to lose it all."

Frank Dufresne wrote as an adventurer. He led people on with sharp, neat, enticing stories of the things he saw, the things he learned, the things which, as a woodsman, he knew. He believed, I am certain, the old carnival adage, "You can't sell 'em popcorn until you get them in under the tent." His astute observations and gritty experiences got them in, and the popcorn he sold them was the truth about what was happening to their world then, just halfway through the 1960s.

When *No Room for Bears* was first published toward the end of 1965, readers of nature books and conservationists in general began telling each other about a fresh, clear voice from Alaska. Word spread, and the book developed a kind of cult following. Alaska seemed so far away in 1965. It indeed was the "last frontier," a wilderness where eggs cost a dollar apiece and there were few roads. They used dog teams for traveling in Alaska, and people could walk away from camp and never be seen again.

This place called Alaska was wild. We had seen pictures, we knew it had majestic scale, and there were bears. There were Kodiak bears, Peninsula bears, polar bears, black bears, blue glacier bears (that were really black bears) and cinnamon-colored black bears too, grizzly bears, and lots of Alaskan brown bears.

Some scientists said there were sixty-four distinct species of the brown bears alone, and some said all of them except the black bears and polar bears belonged to one species. We didn't know who was right, of course, but bears there were, in great and grand variety.

Then there was that voice, that Dufresne fellow in the North-land speaking out with a voice of reason: "The wilderness is being defiled. Soon there won't be any room in the world for bears." It's easy to ignore warning voices if they are shrill, given to hyperbole, or seem uninformed. Frank Dufresne's voice was none of these things. He made sense and clearly he knew what he was talking about, and so we listened. *No Room for Bears* is still exciting, its cautions are still valid.

Alaska has gotten closer, and they have built a few more roads. They have spilled oil, and the airline schedules are more user-friendly. But the bears are still there. I believe this is in part because Frank Dufresne appealed to our consciences and educated us. It is good to have the book back in print so it can give pleasure and do its work for another generation of readers of the wild. And the bears? They need its courage and its reason no less now than then.

Roger Caras
Thistle Hill Farm
Maryland

¶ Preface: Bear Island

The most amazing concentration and assortment of brown and grizzly bears on the planet today is on Admiralty Island in Southeastern Alaska, no more than twenty miles from the capital city of Juneau. Airborne travelers to and from Seattle daily fly over its contrasting white peaks and dark green forests in which dwells a grizzly or brown bear for approximately every one of its 1,600 square miles. The famous Inside Passage steamer channel separating Admiralty Island from the mainland glaciers is close enough so that passengers on deck occasionally spot deer and bears through their binoculars, and sometimes even glimpse a rare trumpeter swan winging white against the timbered slopes.

The 100-mile-long island, averaging 16 miles wide, is convoluted with innumerable bays, coves and inlets, and drained by clear, fast-flowing rivers filled seasonally with six kinds of trout and salmon. Lakes and beaver ponds wink back at airline passengers, and the high, interior country is clothed in green meadows. The island is beautiful, almost park-like in character, and for many years one group of Americans after another has tried to have its unique scenic and wildlife values held in trust for future generations to enjoy. Because Admiralty's abounding fish and game resources are a resource needing to be cropped to hold them in bounds, National Park status is seldom recommended. Instead, it is urged that the region be managed with an eye to its recreational features in the years that lie beyond our own scope of life. Since Admiralty Island is a part of the National Forest system belonging to all the people of the United States, the way has always been open for direct action by the Federal Government. A stroke of the pen by the President, by the Secretary of the Interior or of Agriculture, could do it.

Hopeful signs that such preferential treatment might be considered were in evidence as early as the mid-1930's. In the pamphlet, "Bear Management Plan for Admiralty Island," issued jointly by the old Alaska Game Commission and the Alaska Branch of the U.S. Forest Service (for which I did considerable leg work among the bears), the browns and grizzlies were given high priority. Recently, the Forest Service appeared to be reaffirming its abiding interest in the big bears and other wildlife and fishery values on Admiralty. A late handbook of the Forest Service, in fact, contains these words:

Visitors and onlookers from the other 49 States will be concerned with the preservation of the wildlife, scenery and wilderness for which Alaska is famous. If and when this last frontier is conquered by "progress" something precious in the minds of the people will have died.

At the exact time when these fine phrases appeared in the Forest Service handbook, a resident of Petersburg, Alaska, who had spent many years cruising around Admiralty Island, and tramping up and down its river banks, was reporting conditions in shocking contrast.

In an article called "Last Chance for Admiralty" in the May, 1964, issue of FIELD & STREAM magazine, registered guide Ralph W. Young said that when he visited a logging camp in Whitewater Bay on the west side of the island, *the ruination of the beautiful wilderness was beyond belief*. He said that trees were being cut to the banks of the creek, leaving no cover at all. He said that giant 500-year-old spruces were being felled and left to rot. He said that erosion would be massive in a few years. He said that the stream emptying into Whitewater Bay was "a raging torrent of mud."

Immediately, the Forest Service issued a denial of the charges, and in so doing made a number of statements that Ralph Young in turn challenged. Among the charges and counter charges, certain statements stand like tall trees after a storm:

That the actual living room and food supply of the brown-grizzly bears on Admiralty Island could be reduced drastically if logging continues at current rates and methods.

That the Forest Service intends to pursue its present policy.

That a majority of Alaska's politicians and business houses, confronted with a sagging economy and the urgent need to convert raw materials into cash, favor continued logging on Admiralty, and turn a deaf ear to pleas of "outsiders" to save the bears.

That a preponderance of citizens across the United States would like to have this island in the National Forest system managed for its unique bear populations and other fish and wildlife recreational features.

That local fishermen are angrily protesting the needless destruction of salmon-spawning rivers by the type of logging now permitted by the U.S. Forest Service on Admiralty Island.

That Admiralty is an important wintering area for the rare trumpeter swan, and may hold a few nesting pairs in summer.

That where grizzlies are already as highly concentrated as

on Admiralty Island, further reduction of food and habitat could lead to tragic consequences.

Just before writing the final pages of this book, I made a return trip by small airplane to Admiralty Island to revisit the scene of the opening chapter. Thirty-two years earlier the great bear man Hosea Sarber and I had watched a family of grizzlies in these primitive evergreen forests as it gathered at a diamond-clear river filled with migrating salmon.

For years the perfection of the scene had been etched in my memory—the waterfall over which the otters had tobogganed with gay exuberance; the playful yearling grizzly; the mother with twin cubs nursing at her breasts; the big boar who tried to scare us away with his fierce *whuffs*; the old Methuselah bear, gray with age, standing at the foot of the falls like an "end of the trail" painting.

As I sat buckled in the little float plane yawing like a kite in the air currents, I had but to close my eyes to bring back the sight and sound of that moment again—the mewing of the short-billed gulls; the croaking of the ravens as they hopped about trying to steal salmon scraps from the bears; the white-headed eagles screaming from the snags; the dark green of the forest primeval. I thought I would remember the beauty of it forever.

Ralph Young, strapped alongside, nudged me with his elbow. "There it is!" he shouted above the engine chatter. "Don't you see it?" The plane tipped on its side. "It's right below," said Young gesturing downward with his thumb. "That's the valley you and Hosea Sarber called the prettiest place you ever saw."

It wasn't pretty any more. It was as ugly as only man could make it, defiling a wilderness. The entire green valley of

towering virgin trees had been felled by logging crews, dragged
down to the bay, and towed away to the pulp mill. Now, there
was only mud—miles of it—a slithering sea of sloppy muck
in which nothing could live, and the river itself was fouled
beyond imagination. It looked as lifeless as the aftermath of
an atomic bomb explosion.

We dropped low, skimming the cruel desolation, hoping to
find a grizzly track. We didn't see any. The pilot finished his
low run and asked if we wanted to look around some more.
Ralph shook his head. It wasn't any use. The grizzlies had fled
to another watershed, crowding in on other bears. Soon they
would have to flee into another patch of shrinking forest, and
later to still another—if they could find it.

"Only a man in a big chair back in Washington can save
Admiralty now . . ." Ralph Young started to say, then lapsed
into silence. I knew what was in his mind, because it was in
mine, too. The grizzlies and the recreational beauty of this
famous island had been measured against saw-logs and found
wanting. It was the story of the West all over again. There
wasn't any room for the bears.

F.D.
1965

❡ Contents

No Room for Bears

q   Grizzly Habitat

The fire had burned low that night the grizzly came into camp. Hosea had fallen asleep and I, who should have been on guard, had done the same. In the darkness a smoldering spruce log burned in two and collapsed with a crash. Showers of sparks flew like fireflies into the treetops and a tongue of flame licked at the misty forest. I came awake with a start. No more than a pebble's toss away stood one of the biggest grizzly bears I had ever seen.

As I groped for my gun I could feel my throat pounding. Maybe I should call out to Hosea, I thought, and then there wasn't any need. The guide was already awake. Silently, he rolled to a sitting posture, his hands gripping his .375 rifle ready for action.

"Heave some more wood on the fire," he said quietly, not taking his eyes off the bear. "Stir it up real good."

He didn't have to tell me that trouble had arrived, and that what happened next could be very important to a couple of deer hunters. Whatever it might be, we'd asked for it. We'd started down from one of Admiralty Island's snow peaks in late afternoon, following a deeply rutted bear trail used by the brown giants for centuries. The sun went down and its afterglow, which we'd been relying on to light us down the final three miles to our anchored gas boat, was suddenly blotted out by a rolling fog bank that hung like drapes from the low limbs of the evergreens. It had blinded us in a moment. With visibility reduced to arm's length we were bogged down for the night amidst the heaviest concentration of brown and grizzly bears in all Alaska. We'd made it even worse. We'd baited ourselves with prime grizzly food. Dripping blood-scent all the way down from the high meadows and now spread-eagled across a downed log between us were two freshly-killed Sitka bucks.

Hosea had accepted the situation calmly. While we could still see enough to grope our way among the massive tree trunks, he led the way to a windfallen spruce. He pried off some bark slabs, reached underneath for a handful of dry splinters, and touched off a fire. In its growing light we gathered heaps of fallen branches to last us through the dark hours. We knew that during the night several grizzlies would be using their trail to visit the salmon spawning streams down in the valley. They'd smell the venison and they'd want it. How far would they go to take it away from us? We'd soon find out.

The big grizzly had reared to full height to peer down at us across the firelight, its massive head swaying from side to side as it studied us carefully. Its eyes, shining like red lights as they reflected the flame, showed neither anger nor fear; only intense curiosity, as the huge beast tried to figure out what two humans were doing in its woods after dark. It had never encountered a man at such close range, and certainly not in the nighttime when the advantage was on its side. It was making up its mind. I remembered something Hosea had once told me; that a wild grizzly is not only one of the most intelligent of all beasts, but it recognizes man as its sole challenger for supremacy.

"Give a grizzly a chance to look you over, to catch a snootful of human scent; give it the time and opportunity to make a dignified retreat," Hosea had counseled, adding, "It might go away, or it might attack." But the guide wasn't talking now. The bear was too close. It could be on us in a split second, and our chances for stopping it cold were none too good in the flickering firelight.

Like some other bear men, Hosea often talked to the grizzlies when he was trying to gauge their moods, not loud but in the moderate tones one might use to placate a barking dog. "Take it easy, big boy," he called out now. "You better mosey on down to the creek and fill up on salmon. You can't have our deer." In an aside to me he added, "While he's standing still I could take him through the brains and end all this, but maybe we won't have to. Maybe he'll listen to reason."

The bear was, indeed, listening. Its ears were cocked. Its black, rubbery nose was thrust forward as its flaring nostrils sniffed the air. The tantalizing aroma of deer flesh told it to charge. The curtain of fire told it to go away. The sight and sound of man confused it. Dropping to all fours the grizzly padded into the eerie shadows and started circling around the burning limbs. So far it had uttered no sound, but in the damp gloom of the big trees I could hear the click of teeth as it champed its jaws nervously.

"That's not a good sign," observed Hosea. "Better stoke up that fire again." I did, and the grizzly's hairy rump looked like a haystack as it faded away in the fog-filled night.

A half hour passed. A yearling weighing 300 or 400 pounds came shambling down the trail, stopped to look us over, then moved gingerly on its way. Not far behind came a female with two small cubs. The cubs sat up like a pair of coons, fascinated by the campfire, all eyes and ears and questing noses toward the first human beings they had ever seen. They started forward to do a better job of it and were cuffed soundly on their backsides by the mother. Squalling loudly, the cubs fled down the trail. We could hear the female scolding long after they'd vanished into the inky forest.

There was no sign of the giant grizzly; only the slow drip-drip of moisture falling off the trees and the hiss of a drop hitting the embers. The rhythm of it made me sleepy again. Following a long day of climbing and backpacking my eyelids were heavy, and I told Hosea now was as good time as any for me to take a nap. Hosea said to go ahead and he'd try to keep a watch on things. "You know," he added casually, "that grizzly is still out there looking at us."

I decided to stay awake. Hosea's remark had refilled the night with danger. Hopefully, I suggested that the bear had gone on down the trail to join the others at the salmon riffles. Hosea didn't answer for twenty minutes, then all he said was "Look!" My eyes followed his pointing finger to a pair of red-hot coals glowing in the dark.

Though the guide held his rifle at ready and cautioned me to do the same—but not to fire unless he did—Hosea said he didn't think this was an attack situation. He reasoned that if the grizzly already had the deer in possession it would fight to death to keep it. Now the bear was in the position of being the aggressor so it might be different. "There's a code of behavior among these hairy brutes." Under his week-old stubble Hosea managed a wry grin. "I wish I knew it better."

The two live coals floated several feet higher in the velvety blackness, and I knew the grizzly had reared on its hind feet to examine us again. Then, suddenly, the lights dropped and blinked out.

"Now what?" I whispered.

Looking back on it now, I don't really think Hosea was surprised at what happened next. I think he'd been expecting something like it all that night. Suddenly, the ebony stillness was shattered by horrendous roars. The awful bawls echoed ventriloquially through the fog and seemed to shake the very ground where we stood. Again and again came the frightful outbursts, the more alarming because I was finally able to pinpoint the source. The grizzly had moved and now it was directly behind us.

I don't know what the bear expected us to do—possibly bolt into the forest and leave it in charge of the two dead bucks. That's what another lesser bear might have done at the bellowed commands. I, too, felt like running but knew better than to leave the campfire. Hastily, I joined Hosea on the other side, and with a wall of flame between us and the grizzly once more, we waited with thumbs pushing against the safeties on our rifles, ready as we possibly could be for a charge.

In the hair trigger silence every flickering shadow took on the shape of a bear. Minutes passed, then hours with nothing to break the tension. At daybreak each of us shouldered his deer siwash-fashion, with the front legs toggled through the hamstrings and with rifles resting across the racks made by the outthrust hind legs. The deep pad prints led down along a steep hogback. Hosea, showing the way, halted and pointed below to a salmon spawning river rippling under the hemlocks and devil's-club. A female bear and two smallish cubs were sharing a fish on a gravel bar, and a fair-size yearling was romping in the spray of a waterfall, more playful than hungry. Hosea kept waiting for something else to show and finally it did. A giant male came swaggering out of a tunnel through some salmonberry brush into the river and picked up a humpbacked salmon in its teeth. He shook it viciously.

"Well, the bears are all down there," observed the guide. "Want to go down for a closer look?"

"Some other time," I said.

"Some other time" turned out to be the next day. With our fat Sitka bucks safely hung in the rigging; fortified by a restful sleep on the gently rocking gas boat, Hosea and I rowed ashore

in the dark moments before dawn. Together, we dragged the
light skiff atop squishy kelp bulbs and over squirting clams to
the high-tide line, made the painter fast to a barnacled rock
and started trudging across an open meadow shoulder-deep in
wild ryegrass. Because our man-scent would carry upstream,
we made a wide detour before cutting straight into the river to
hit a spot several yards above the steep falls beyond which no
salmon could migrate.

We moved cautiously down in our rubber-bottomed pacs to
a huge fallen tree overlooking the cataract and settled ourselves behind it for an all day vigil. Though Hosea carried his
heavy rifle—he seldom went ashore on Admiralty Island without it—he would not use it unless we were charged. We'd try
for a few camera shots, but mostly we were here on this primi-
tively beautiful Southeastern Alaska stream to observe the
ways of a grizzly with a salmon. We didn't have long to wait.

Across the river and up the hogback on the old bear trail a
rust-colored sow bear with twin cubs stood looking down. Had
they seen us? The bears answered our question. One cub after
another came sliding and tumbling eagerly down the steep
incline, followed at a more sedate pace by the mother. They
whisked out of sight in a thicket and a moment later we saw
them splashing water in front of us within a hundred feet. Like
a doting parent, the female watched her whining youngsters
wade up to their necks in the river, grabbing at passing fish.
When they turned to mother pleading for help, the female
strode out into the water, lowered her head completely out of
sight in the current and came up with a salmon dangling from
her jaws. Followed by the squealing cubs, she bore her catch
out on a gravel bar, laid a paw on its head, and with one slash
of her teeth ripped the skin completely off one side. Bickering
like little demons, the furry balls sunk their baby teeth into
the soft pink flesh. When they had stripped one side bare the
mother yanked the remaining hide off and joined her children
for breakfast.

In the early sunlight a flock of short-billed gulls came flying upriver from the tide flats, screaming and hovering over the bear family, swooping daintily to snatch bits of salmon out of the very jaws of death. A swish of wings brought a black raven to the scene. It danced a lively jig on its feet as it hopped in and out, narrowly missing angry paw swipes and gnashing teeth, feinting here and grabbing there for tidbits. More bird trouble continued to arrive. With full daylight came more gulls, bold glaucous-winged varieties strong enough to make off with the entire skeleton of the salmon. The mother fought off the winged pests for a while, then planted herself squarely over the picked bones, head waving from side to side as if in deep thought. A solution came to mind. Without a further glance at the haggling birds she sloshed out into the river and fished out another salmon. She was holding it in her jaws when she suddenly grew tense. She'd sensed danger.

Squatting in the water the she-bear swung her eyes from the waterfall across the log in front of Hosea and me, then continued to scan the river bank before leading her cubs out of sight into a low jungle of giant hellebore and alders. For a while the gravel bar was deserted save for the birds. We had the feeling that other grizzlies, hidden as we were, were surveying the river cautiously before venturing out into the open. Whether they had sensed human presence, or were maintaining a wary respect toward their own kind, we couldn't tell. In the end it was the yearling who broke the spell.

With utter disregard for proper bear behavior, the youngster came galloping down the hillside with all the grace of a boy in a potato-sack race, ripped through the underbrush, and somewhat dazed by the buffeting, splash-landed in the middle of the pool. In frantic alarm at the watery explosion a flurry of salmon tried to jump straight up the waterfall, fell back, and when one of them drifted downstream, the yearling recovered enough to clap its jaws over the spent fish. Surprised at its own smartness, the yearling looked around as though expecting applause. But what it got was an angry *whuff*!

The half-ton giant behind it had slipped through the timber without a sound. Now, with one peremptory snort it took charge of the fishing hole. The chastened yearling slunk away with its salmon, and the female kept her cubs out of sight while the big boar proceeded to catch and eat two salmon before stretching itself on the sand to rest. In a few moments yearling, mother, and cubs came out of hiding though careful to keep their distance from his majesty. I could see now what Hosea meant by the grizzly's code. Pretending not to notice one another, the great carnivores shared the pool and took their turns fishing. I held up a hand with fingers spread to denote five bears in this one spot. Silently, Hosea did the same, then extended the index finger on his other hand. Six bears! With his thumb the guide motioned toward the base of the falls. It was behind my right shoulder, and the distance couldn't possibly be more than fifteen feet away!

With infinite care I turned my head and rose high enough to peer over the waterfall. Below me was the oldest living bear I have ever seen, a Methuselah among grizzlies. Its long muzzle was hoary with age, and its matted coat was like a heap of rags. It was deeply swaybacked; its head hung low. It stood close enough to the falls for the water to keep it drenched. The massive front paws rested in a shallow basin filled to the brim with wriggling salmon that had failed to clear the waterfall and fallen into a natural trap among the rocks. Though it was surely the choicest stand on the river, not one of the other bears had come near it all day. It was grandpa's private fishing hole.

The odds against this grizzly patriarch surviving the heavy snowfall of the Admiralty Island winter must have been great. Yet, like the other bears, it had come pushing out of its den in the high crags in April or May to plod downward across melting drifts in search of a strong cathartic to loosen the resinous plug that had sealed its intestines shut for almost half a year. The remedy had been the violently pungent root of the skunk cab-

bage, snow lily bulbs, and helebore stalks. Like the other grizzlies, Methuselah had doubtless snuffled and pawed along the
bottom of snowslides for the carrion of winter-killed deer and
lesser creatures, and even the carcasses of less fortunate bears.
Down on the Admiralty beaches it had eaten enormous quantities of tender spring grass seasoned with crabs, clams, and
beetles secured by turning over boulders along the bared flats
at low tide. All this to still the hunger rumblings in its pendulous belly until nature's bounty filled the rivers with the
annual coming of the silver hordes, five kinds of salmon hom-
ing to their spawning streams from thousands of miles at sea
to perform a miracle of migration. More than any other factor
the salmon had given Admiralty Island a grizzly and brown
bear population density unequaled anywhere else on earth.
One bear to each square mile! Five times more bears than
people!

Toward the noon hours grizzly activity slowed along the
river. I was dozing in the warm sun when Hosea nudged me.
The big male bear had lifted its head and was looking directly
at the log behind which we were hidden. I didn't think it had
seen us because we were completely screened by the lacy foli-
age of a hemlock branch. Nor had we uttered so much as a
whisper to one another. What we feared most was a tiny whiff
of our hated man-scent eddying back against the breeze. Was
this what had happened? After a long stare, the big grizzly
rolled to its feet and came swaggering out of the shadows
toward us. At the water's edge it reared up on its giant frame,
looking ten feet tall as it peered across the river. Then it
dropped heavily down on its forefeet, swung about, and padded into the dark shadows. When it failed to show up again
I glanced behind our lookout with some apprehension, won-
dering if we were about to witness another flanking maneu-
ver like this same bear had tried two nights before on the
mountainside.

Hosea's finger touched me on the shoulder to turn me

around. The big male was back again at the same spot. This time it came wading halfway across the river, and with water running off its hooked claws lifted up and gave us another hard look. Out of the corner of my eyes I saw the guide's fingers tighten once more on his rifle. Then, suddenly, the heat was off for a moment at least. A salmon drifted past and the bear couldn't resist picking it up.

But we knew something was wrong when the beast bit a chunk out of the salmon's back and then dropped the limp carcass on the gravel bar. It paid no attention when a bald eagle flopped heavily from a low snag to claim the spoils. Screaming gulls and croaking ravens gathered to harass the king of birds at its feast.

There was no sign of the mother and cubs and the yearling. Something had caused them to vacate. As the big male followed them into the forest gloom the hackles along its shoulders stood stiffly erect. For the first time that day the guide spoke. "We'd better keep our eyes peeled. The time to worry is when you can't see 'em."

I raised up to look over the log again and it was reassuring to see Methuselah at the same old stand under the falls. His sagging back was damp with spray. Salmon slithered over his paws and under his gray nose waiting to be picked up. But there was no evidence that the aged grizzly had eaten, and the thought came to me that maybe, like the other bears, he was beginning to tire of a straight diet of salmon. The same thing happened every summer. After a spell of fish, the bears commenced mixing the pink flesh with blueberries, gathering the berries first along the beach where they ripened earliest, then working their way into the mountains for the late harvest that lasted until denning time.

Although Hosea and I now began conversing aloud there was no indication that the hoary old timer heard us, or at least not well enough to identify it as a human sound. Undoubtedly, he was deaf and when he swung his head downstream for a moment his eyes seemed to be glazed with a bluish film. It had taken Methuselah five years to attain adult size. Had this now been multiplied by the factor of seven to produce the bear life span of thirty-five? Was the old giant living his last summer?

Paying the aged grizzly no more attention than if he were a moss-grown boulder, an otter came sliding over the brink of the falls and plunged into the bubbling water twenty feet below. I watched the glistening streak of its long body along the bottom, fluid as mercury before belly-whumping over the shallow riffles around the bend of the river. Soon another otter came along to follow the exact procedure. The salmon, which had parted to let the exuberant pair through, resumed their spawning. With furious energy the females used their tails to thrash out redds in the gravel, then squeezed out a string of pink, pea-sized eggs to be fertilized with whitish clouds of milt from the quivering males. Handsome Dolly Varden trout darted around each spawning pair to snap up the free-floating waste eggs. As each salmon exhausted its roe sac, it drifted dying in the current, easy prey for the bears when they came back to feed again at dusk.

When they did, Hosea and I would be back aboard the gas boat bucking the tide for home. Before we left I took a long look at one of the most perfect grizzly habitats left in the world. I wondered how much longer it would last.

¶ **The Twenty-fifth Bear**

Ever since the appearance of their ancestors on earth, man and bears have been at odds. Beginning in the Pleistocene when giant cave bears towered over every other predator—of which man must be reckoned as one—our low-browed grandfathers were forced to cope with shaggy-haired beasts who stood twice as tall and outweighed them ten to one. For half a million years it was the bear, not man, who dominated the wilds, and it continued to hold the upper edge until the development of high-powered rifles within the past two hundred years.

In this short period—the blink of an eye in time—some of the bears have not adjusted their thinking to man's sudden supremacy. Some of them still believe they can whip any man in a fair fight, and that they have every right to run him out of the dwindling wilderness. My friend, Hosea, the greatest bear student I ever knew, used to say that about one grizzly out of twenty-five is ready to do battle against a human for reasons best known to themselves. "Unfortunately," Hosea would add slyly, "they don't wear numbers on their backs like football players so you never can be sure when you've met the twenty-fifth bear."

I knew what he meant, because I had searched unsuccessfully for one of these "twenty-fifth" bears. It had all started when a forest ranger was mauled to death by a grizzly while cruising timber on Admiralty Island. His death was to start another public outcry to remove all protection on Alaskan bears, put a bounty on the killers, poison them, get rid of them all. Of the several fatal attacks and maimings of humans by grizzlies, the case of the forest ranger was to create the most attention.

But, of course, the ranger would never know about this furor. All he knew was that a bear lurked nearby in the rain forest and that he would take no chances with it. The minute he laid eyes on it he would drop it in its tracks. He couldn't afford to be careless. It was too dark; the bear would be too close. So the ranger had made up his mind to shoot quickly if the animal showed the first sign of a fight.

Evidence of its nearness was clear to a woodsman of the forest ranger's experience. There was the much used wallow hole filled with still roily water, and the huge padded prints in the soft mud alongside. A spruce tree near the game trail down which the ranger and his unarmed helper were traveling had been shredded of its bark as high as he could reach with the muzzle of his rifle. Matted brown hair clung to the oozing pitch. In the trail itself was the real payoff—a half-eaten salmon fresh out of the creek.

The ranger held up his hand in silent, tense warning to his young aid, who was following close with a bulky packload of camp supplies. The rifle came out of the crook of his left arm; his right index finger slid inside the trigger guard, and his thumb pressed hard against the safety lever. This might have to be quick.

He listened carefully. There was no sound except that of their own heavy breathing and the flop-flop of spawning coho salmon in the small stream that ran around the bottom of the knoll on which they stood. Both men were dead sure now that the bear was near; that it must have sensed them and had chosen to stand its ground. You get to feel things like this when your job is scouting timber on the primitive forest lands of Admiralty Island with its estimated population of 1,600 bears!

Later, when I talked with the young backpacker, he told me he saw the grizzly first, and hissed an excited warning to the ranger. Silent as a shadow, the bear had risen off its bed between three closely growing hemlocks and faced them with lowered head. The distance was twenty feet. For a half minute the small eyes stared at them. The helper said he would never forget; they were like two red marbles. He saw the black, rubbery lips separate to bare yellowed teeth.

At the crash of the rifle the young backpacker told me he jumped off the knoll and went rolling and clawing down through prickly devil's-club to the creek bottom. Wrestling out of his pack, he scrambled to a smallish tree and swarmed up until he reached a point level with the knoll-top. The ranger was not in sight. The bear was bouncing about insanely with movements so fast it was all a blur to the helper's eyes. When the beast backed away for a second he saw the ranger face down on the ground trying to push himself up with his arms. The helper got one horrified glimpse of clothing ripped to rags, of bloody, gaping wounds. Then the bear rushed in again, roaring and mauling and shaking the man until he was limp.

The helper said he didn't recall too clearly what then happened. At the sight of his partner's stricken body, he dropped to the ground and climbed up the knoll hoping in some vague way to recover the rifle and get in a telling shot with it. But when he reached the ranger he knew it was too late. The bear had vented its rage and fled the scene. There was nothing to do except try to bandage the awful wounds, build a campfire, and keep a death watch through the ensuing night.

He had trouble locating the rifle. A blow of the bear's paw had spun it from the ranger's hands and sent it flying far into the brush. It had been fired once, the empty brass case ejected, and a fresh cartridge fed halfway into the firing chamber. Here was mute testimony of the terrific speed of the charge, because the ranger had been fairly adept in the handling of firearms. He must have had less than a second from the time he fired the first hurried shot until the beast struck him down.

When the young helper showed me the spot a few days later it was our hope to destroy the bear before it attacked another human. An Indian tracker picked up the footprints and we followed them into the high meadows above timber line before they faded out. There was no sign of blood. A year elapsed before Hosea came to see me with what he said was a hunch. He reasoned that if the bear had not been wounded too severely, with the passage of time it might return to its old fishing hole.

It was a rainy, gloomy day on the 16th of October—a year to the day since the attack—when Hosea left his gas boat at the mouth of the river. Before rowing ashore in a small skiff, he instructed his boating companion to wait aboard until noon of the next day before attempting to follow his trail up the river. "I was up against a wily, dangerous grizzly," said the guide later. "Having once been stung by a rifle bullet and having killed the man who fired the shot, that bear would have a savage reception ready for the next human to invade its domain." But Hosea had confidence in his own ability and told his shipmate to listen for shooting late in the afternoon. If there had been a successful encounter he would fire three fast shots.

In the lower stretches of the river Hosea saw almost no sign of bear that day. The early runs of humpback and dog salmon were over and the carcasses of spawned-out fish had been washed into the bay by heavy fall rains. But up in the narrow headwaters Hosea knew that the late spawning cohos would still be threshing out their redds in the gravel, and that each favorite site would have its quota of bears. He saw two yearlings searching the empty riffles ahead, and waited until they went into the timber before proceeding. He had no intention of letting them squall an alarm to the bears upstream.

At noon the guide reached the forks where the particular stream he was seeking joined the main river. There had been dozens of small tributaries, but Hosea was too good a woodsman to stray off the penciled directions I—as director of the Game Commission—had made for him. As he told me later, he found part of a rusted kerosene lantern abandoned by the litter-bearing party the year before, and noted places where the blueberry bushes had been axed away to let the carriers through with their lifeless burden. As he neared the scene of the killing, Hosea said, he became extremely cautious, stopping to test the wind and sometimes standing motionless for minutes at a time. It was a spooky sort of place under the canopy of giant trees, fog-shrouded and dim. Few men would care to venture alone here to match wits with one of the wiliest and most savage of all wild game.

The distance was now less than a quarter of a mile to the knoll. Hosea deliberately waited for the late afternoon hours in the hope of catching the bear out in the stream where he could spy it first. When he could see the pool, there were parts of salmon on the bank where a bear had eaten its fill. Was it the same bear? As Hosea eased lightly past the deep imprints of a grizzly, its fetid odor hung heavy in the dank air, and he knew he was very close. In spite of his long experience among these bears, Hosea admitted to a prickly feeling along his scalp. "I could feel death all around me," he confessed.

At the foot of a leaning windfall where a giant hemlock had been uprooted by a windstorm and crashed into the forks of another tree, Hosea stopped to recheck his rifle again. He was carrying his favorite .30-06 sporter, equipped now with receiver sight with open aperture for fast shooting. The cartridges were well-tested 220-grain open point, expanding— deadly if they struck a vital spot. Hosea had heard that the forest ranger had trusted his life to regular Army issue hardpoints, filed square for dumdum effect. The guide had no faith in such makeshift ammunition. Removing first one hand and then the other from the damp gunstock, he wiped them dry against the wool shirt under his light slicker-jacket. His eyes measured the trunk of the windfall, selecting steps among the exposed roots where he could mount in a hurry if need be.

"I'd come far enough," said Hosea. "I'd gambled on the grizzly being at this spot. But now all I heard were cohos in the creek and the drip-drip of rain."

Call it premonition, sixth sense, or what you will, Hosea, who was not in the habit of loading the chamber of his rifle until he was ready to fire, now drew back the bolt and eased a cartridge into firing position. The operation was barely audible —a light, oily *snick*. But it triggered an explosive roar, followed by a crescendo of trumpet-blasts that reverberated through the forest. The spine-chilling outbursts seemed to come from everywhere. The instant he heard them Hosea mounted quickly to the windfall and ran upward until he stood on the leaning trunk fifteen feet above a dense patch of devil's-club. He knew now that the beast had been watching for him. With the hateful scent of man full in its nostrils it had been silently closing in for the attack at the very second Hosea's hunch had caused him to work the bolt of his rifle. Hosea thinks the grizzly still remembered the slight, metallic click that had preceded a rifle blast on another October day.

In its baffled fury the bear thrashed about in the heavy cover trying to flush out the man enemy. By climbing to a point overhead, Hosea had suddenly cut off his fresh scent. Air currents with their tendency to swirl upward were all at once lost to the bear. Looking down on the crazed beast now, there was no longer any doubt in Hosea's mind that this was the grizzly that had taken a man's life. In all his years of working among the bears of Southeastern Alaska he had never witnessed such rage; had never seen a bear so determined to attack. Unable to see its foe, its roars and rapidly ejaculated *chuff-chuff-chuff* of clashing teeth changed to whining eagerness.

Midway in its crashing leaps the bear suddenly froze motionless. A vagrant down-scent had carried Hosea's location to its nose. It rose on hind feet and for ten long seconds looked upward to study the face of the enemy. Hosea's shot was cool, unhurried and accurate. There was no need for a second cartridge. Watching the slumped carcass to make certain it was all over, Hosea retraced his steps to the ground and moved forward to prod the bear in the back of its neck with the toe of his boot. Gripping one of the big, furry ears he swung the bulky head around to look for wounds. Down near the shoulder was a long, healed scar that might have been the near miss of another bullet. The guide's shot had exploded a vertebra to cause instant death.

Telling us about it, Hosea wasn't proud of the achievement. "That grizzly knew I was gunning for him just like the forest ranger had tried to kill him the year before. He was fighting for his life and he knew it." Hosea turned to me with a question: "If you had been the grizzly what would you have done?"

Without waiting for a reply because he was sure what it would have to be, Hosea finished his account of the twenty-fifth bear. He said that night was coming on fast when it was all over. There would be barely time enough to get back to the beach before pitch darkness settled over the wet forest. His partner on the boat would be worried. Turning away from the downed bear, Hosea swung the muzzle of his rifle upward and sent three fast shots crashing through the tree tops.

q The First Bear

The first grizzly bear I ever saw was within sight of the place where its pre-Ice Age ancestors reached the continent of North America from Asia. It was a strikingly handsome cream-colored beast with contrasting chocolate-shaded legs. Its head was broad, dishfaced, and the long fur on its shoulder hump rippled like silk in the Arctic wind. It had come pushing through a clump of willows to face toward Bering Strait where an isthmus once linked Alaska and Siberia. But symbolical as it appeared, the great beast was not looking back over the trail of its sires. It was staring straight into my eyes and the distance was uncomfortably close.

I had been visiting an Eskimo reindeer camp on the shores of Kotzebue Sound and had accompanied a group of native herders while they combed the hinterlands to round up a band of several thousand reindeer. They were moving the semiwild animals slowly down a willow-grown valley toward an exposed beach. The reindeer had already smelled the brine-freighted breeze off the Arctic Ocean and were hurrying to reach its pounding surf, not only to lick at bits of salt-encrusted driftwood but to seek relief in the sea winds from swarms of stinging insects that infest the northern tundra in summer. The clacking of reindeer hoofs, the pig-like grunting of mothers calling to their fawns, and the shouts of the Eskimos rose in a strange cacophony of sound. Suddenly, a wave of terror seemed to sweep through the herd. The frightened deer exploded out of the thickets and in a moment had stampeded over the skyline. Behind them in the shoulder-high brush there was a commotion of unseen creatures, then silence.

Skilrak, the Eskimo chief herder, joined me. I asked him if a wolf had attacked the reindeer. He shook his head. "Wolf cannot kill that quick. This one, I think maybe, is Takuka the yellow bear."

He went on to explain that since he had no gun it would not be smart to search in the willows. "The yellow bear has already killed," he reasoned aloud. "Before it is hungry again we will have the herd at our summer camp." He went shuffling away in his soft-soled mukluks to help his boys gather up the terrified reindeer and once again get them trotting toward the ocean. He motioned for me to follow, but I couldn't resist remaining behind in hopes of glimpsing my first wild grizzly.

It was not long in coming. With stealth I had not thought possible for such a large beast, the bear had left its dead reindeer and crept toward me through the willows without disturbing a leaf. It had taken advantage of a sunken creek bed and followed it to the last clump of brush, and must have been watching me at close range for several seconds before I saw its low-hung head in the shadows. The instant our eyes met the grizzly lifted to its haunches. Its small eyes were like glinting pinpoints. Its big, furry ears were cocked forward, and as its flaring nostrils thrust forward twitching for scent I felt myself reeling backwards as though from actual impact. In my stumbling retreat a very fortunate thing occurred. A gust of wind whipped around my head, picked up a load of scent and carried it to the bear. Now, it was the grizzly's turn to be shocked.

Obviously, it had expected to challenge a rival bear, not a human, because it dropped to all fours and whirled back into cover. I didn't tempt fate by staying near its kill any longer. But brief as the encounter had been, I had seen one of the richest furred and most beautifully marked of all grizzlies. It was the rare tundra bear, descendant of the old world *Ursus arctos,** which in prehistoric times had padded across a land bridge to Alaska. It was the first of a burly clan to set paw on this continent, destined to increase into the tens of thousands and to dominate the American wilderness for centuries to come.

Ursus arctos, better known as the European brown bear, is credited with being the parent of all the 232 types, races, and subspecies of brown and grizzly bears scattered across the northern half of the globe. It existed as long ago as 12 million years in the Pliocene era, sharing the old world with numerous other oddballs, some of which hadn't yet decided whether to turn themselves into wolves or bears. But even these weird-looking creatures were not the first bears to appear on the planet earth.

In Oligocene strata dating back more than 30 million years fragments of skulls and bone splinters had been uncovered that the scientists pored over to produce the skeleton of a primitive mammal called the *Amphicynodon.* It was apparently neither dog nor bear, but something of both with genes of panda, raccoon, coyote, and jackal tossed in to further

---

*Concerning the classification of bears used throughout this book, Dirk Pieter Erdbrink, in his book *A Review of Fossil and Recent Bears of the Old World* (Deventer, 1953: Drukkerig Jan de Lange), simply destroyed our Dr. C. Hart Merriam's multi-varieties in favor of a much tighter system which has now been adopted by most, if not all, biologists in America. Thus, Dr. Merriam's *Euarctos, Thalarctos, etc.,* are now designated under the classification *Ursus.*

mystify the professors. This scrambled beast was succeeded by process of evolution 10 million or more years later in the Miocene by the *Hemicyon,* which has been described as a dog living in the half-ton body of bear. Somewhere in this long-gone era came the *Caphalogale,* scientifically important because paleontologists could at last detect a definite parting of the ways between canines and bears, an exact beginning of the difference that was to separate them for all time. Henceforth, there would be many varieties of dogs and almost as many bears, but never a combination of both under one hide.

The bear portion of this rift began in due time to shape itself into a thing called the *Ursavus.* It took a few million years and the result was a true bear-creature not much bigger than a wolf, found in the Miocene deposits of Austria and France about 15 million years ago. *Ursavus* is believed to be the direct progenitor of the current European brown bear, a most vigorous beast whose family tree sent branches across Germany, Scandinavia, Poland, Russia, China, Syria and way points; then on across Siberia to Alaska and southward into Mexico. But bold as it was, the European brown bear was not the greatest in size. It was forced to live for thousands of years in the shadows of two other bears that will go down in history as the largest four-legged carnivorous mammals ever to inhabit the earth.

One was the long-snouted cave bear of Middle Europe and the other was the short-faced bear of America. Both were gigantic. Our existing bears would have looked like yearling cubs alongside them. Both occurred late enough in the Pleistocene to yield abundant skeletal remains, and one of them was directly associated with man.

The cave bear, *Ursus spelaeus,* lived in a period when the world was balmier than today. The lower part of Europe swarmed with apes, feral dogs, mastodons, rhinoceroses, wild asses, boars, hyenas, and great numbers of lions. None of these beasts were as formidable as the great cave bear. Its enormous frame as reconstructed from bones dug up all the way from the British Isles to and beyond Odessa, Russia, indicates a weight of over a ton. It had a long, heavy, low-slung head. Its bones were massive, and its enormous paws were armed with blunt claws. It was huge, terrifying in appearance.

Neither the time nor the place appeared propitious for human existence, yet our low-browed grandfathers had by now invaded the Pleistocene forests swinging their stone clubs. Nor did their battles with the cave bear monster always end with the crunching of people-bones. Sometimes the Neanderthal man won. In the soot-coated caves where the giant bears retired in winter, in the crude sketches on the rock walls, in the heaps of charred firewood and the cooked bones, the story of their occasional victory over the cave bear may be fairly interpreted.

Here, Alley Oop and his brawny pals had found a sleeping bear. They'd dragged up logs to block the cave entrance and set them afire. They'd hurled brands inside and when the suffocating beast shoved its head outside for a breath of fresh air, they'd pounded its skull with their rock cudgels. The siege may have lasted several days with details of men charged with bringing up more firewood while others hammered away at their roaring adversary, flames highlighting the faces of the Neanderthal people as they fought for their lives and their dinners. When they finally beat the giant to death, women and children gathered to feast for days on the huge carcass. They cracked the heavy bones to suck out the marrow, and with sharpened stones they hacked off the shaggy hide and used it to cover their naked bodies.

In justice to the European cave bear, it is believed not to have been a highly aggressive animal; not at all like the flesh-eating lions of the Pleistocene, which were the worst enemies of all the herbivores as well as of man. The cave bear, in fact, appears to have been a pronounced vegetarian. In the end it was not the Stone Age tribes who ate it off the list of living things. It was the increasing cold weather to which they and many other subtropical animals of that era could not adapt themselves. The last of these cave bear giants passed out of existence about 18,000 B.C.

America's own heavyweight bear champ of all time fought under the name of *Arctodus*. Its fossilized bones and awesome fangs have been found deep in Pleistocene levels from one end of this continent to the other, showing abundant populations dating back many thousands of years. Comparing our present day bears with *Arctodus* would be like putting a common black bear up against a Kodiak brownie. Its snubbed off, somewhat tiger-shaped skull caused it to be named the short-faced bear. It was long-legged and rangy and could probably run with the speed of an express train. Undoubtedly, it was the mightiest carnivorous mammal ever to rule the American scene.

While *Arctodus* remnants have been excavated in such far apart places as the Yukon, Pennsylvania, Kentucky, and Texas, by far the greatest finds have been made in the world-famous California tar pits of Rancho La Brea in Los Angeles County. No other spot has yielded up so many perfect specimens, not only of outsize bruins but of an extraordinary list of other mammals graduated all the way from the mammoth down to a least weasel. Caught in the same sticky trap were giant birds like *Teratornis,* an extinct condor that had a wing-spread of 12 feet and was among the largest known birds of flight. Waterfowl of the same kinds that fly over gunner's blinds today lighted down to fly no more, and so did robins and sparrows. There were turtles, lizards, rattlesnakes, and red-legged frogs, even insects in fine state of preservation.

For a meat-eater like *Arctodus* the California tar pits were a natural cafeteria. Antelope, peccary, and deer were there, though outnumbered by herds of wild horses, camels, tapirs, and enormous longhorned bison that stood 7 feet high at the shoulders. There were giant ground sloths each weighing up to three-quarters of a ton, and mastodons, musk oxen and emperor mammoths. Preying on them was the ferocious sabre-toothed bob-tailed cat known as the *Smilodon,* capable of stabbing an elephant to death with its razor-sharp fangs. Much larger than any living member of the cat family was a sort of jaguar with the Latin name of *Panthera atrox*. Several kinds of bears padded about in search of gore, and packs of heavy-skulled dire wolves swept like pestilence over the area. In this galaxy of fearsome creatures, most of them long vanished from this changing world, *Arctodus* swaggered unchallenged.

But the burly brute strength of *Arctodus* could not save it from the tar pools of Rancho La Brea. As the grazing animals ventured too close and became mired in the viscous sands, predators rushed in to tear them apart and were soon gripped by the same gluey substance. Amid the horrid screaming and bellowing of madly struggling beasts, the giant short-faced bear was itself stuck like a bug on a sheet of flypaper.

By seizing and holding entire carcasses in a remarkable state of preservation for up to a half million years, Rancho La Brea contributed knowledge unobtainable from any other source. Among other data was information enabling scientists to trace the devious trails of the bear species that wandered across the face of both Americas before the dawn of human history.

There were three types of bears bogged down in the asphalt beds of Los Angeles County. First was the giant *Arctodus,* linked with a smaller short-faced variety called *Tremarctos* out of which may have sprung the timid spectacled bear of the South American Andes Mountains. There was also a black bear not much different from the panhandlers of Yellowstone Park. Finally, there was a grizzly closely resembling the famous California golden bear, which was rifle-balled into extinction within the memory of living man.

Today, in all the world, only seven distinct kinds of bears survive. It seems strange to surmise—as many naturalists have—that after 25,000,000 years of dominant life on this planet, they may practically all be wiped out of feral existence within the next century; that succeeding generations of humans will know the bears only by peering at stuffed hides in museums.

☊ The Odd Bears

I had never encountered so much ice in all my Alaska travels as on an April day when Joe John, the Indian seal hunter, throttled down the engine on his little gas boat and chugged cautiously into an unnamed fjord at the head of Yakutat Bay. Bergs from the size of baseballs to the size of battleships studded the green water, and on all sides walls of crumbling glaciers towered sheer into the sky for hundreds of feet. The rumble of falling ice chunks was continuous. Now and then an enormous blue slab would split off the face of the glacier and topple slow motion into the fjord with thunderous roars like an artillery barrage.

Here and there between the converging rivers of ice marching down from the high peaks to break off into the sea were islands of scoured rocks, some of them clutching stunted spruce trees and berry bushes in their crevices. On the loftiest of these Joe John pointed to a family of mountain goats; above them circled a pair of bald eagles. As I stood in the bow of the little sealing boat, pike-pole in hand, fending off the bergs, hair seals popped their glistening heads up on all sides. Flocks of pearl-gray terns with scarlet beaks daintily plucked needle-fish from the surface. With engine barely turning over, we drifted and shoved our way to a sheltered cove miraculously free of floating ice. Here Joe John would shoot a deckload of seals for hides and oil while I tried to scramble ashore where possibly no man had ever walked.

There was a push-up of silt at the water's edge barely large enough to beach the skiff. There was also a half-eaten fish and around it a smattering of the tiniest bear tracks I ever saw. They led away under an overhanging shelf of blue ice and through a boulder slide where I had no chance to follow. After trying vainly to scale the perpendicular ice and granite barrier, I rowed back to the gas boat where the Indian waited impatiently to start gathering his seals. As he sculled away, rifle in hand, I uncased my binoculars and began exploring from the deck. I must have glassed across the same ledge a dozen times before I spotted something alive—alive and incredible! It was a bear cub no bigger than a house cat and its color was blue! The wee creature, with enormous curiosity, looked down from the ramparts of its castle at the first human it had ever seen, and in a moment it was joined by two of its litter mates. One of the furry sprites was brown, the other black.

The report of Joe John's .30-30 rifle scattered the rare family. As the cubs of assorted hues whisked into a slot between the rocks, I caught a glimpse of the mother hurrying them along. She looked to be not much larger than a St. Bernard dog and she was coal black.

From the time the first bear-like forms appeared on this planet back in the dim Oligocene they have always been subject to much individual variation, as though nature could never quite settle for a single model. The current glacier bear, *Ursus emmonsi,* is an example of these continuing evolutionary changes. It has been identified as a specialized offshoot of the common American black bear trapped against a precipitous stretch of the Southeastern Alaska coast in the ice age, dwarfed by rigorous living and scanty food supplies, doing its best to grow a fur coat to match its icy and granite background. It has the most restricted range of any bear, and has the fewest numbers—at least those with the odd maltese coloring which has given some of them the name of "blue bear."

They have been called a race on the brink of joining discarded species of the past. The skull is weak, the dentition inferior. Today, there are only a dwindling few glacier bears in the Cape St. Elias area, Yakutat Bay, head of Excursion Inlet, and possibly in the ice-locked canyons at the source of Ford's Terror and Tracy Arm. They are beautiful, very timid, and their small padded feet are pattering on the thin ice of extermination.

South of the glacier bear's last stand, across the international boundary, is another black bear variation with the strangest colorations of them all. I was trolling in the salmon-teeming salt waters off Gribble Island when a brother angler, a cheechako from the States, hailed me to announce that he had just seen a polar bear. Now, a polar bear on this warm, rain-soaked island off the British Columbia shoreline would be more than 1100 miles south of its designated range along the Arctic coast, a record to end all records, so I was interested. On our way to the scene, the angler changed his story to "white" bear, and in this he was right. There wasn't a dark spot on the beast. But it wasn't a polar bear; it was a white black bear!

Salmon guides at the fishing resort expressed no surprise at the anomaly. "We've got 'em all shades," they told us laconically. "White, yellow, brown; most any fancy paint job you want to see."

When I called on the veteran Game Commissioner Frank Butler at his Vancouver office he added more information about this little known bear. A majority of Kermode bear specimens, he said, were black, but some were startling orange, some yellow with dark stripes down the back, some were chestnut red. He added there might be still more combinations of color he hadn't heard about in *Ursus kermodei.*

The small size and the tendency to produce a "Joseph's coat of many colors" indicates a very close kinship between British Columbia's beachcombing Kermode bear and the Alaska glacier bear, though the Kermode type is easier to find. With Princess Royal Island off Kitimat Inlet as the center, its habitat extends from the headwaters of the Nass River southward almost to Bella Coola in a wild region of dark green timber, bald rocks and hanging glaciers. Any beast that tries to play the chameleon against such a spectacular backdrop might well end up by looking like a Kermode bear.

A South American beast may hold title to the "oldest small bear" in the New World. The spectacled bear is the only likely survivor of the giant short-faced bear, *Tremarctos,* that ruled both Americas during the long gone Pleistocene. To find one of these little bears at home today a man must journey all the way to Ecuador, Peru, Bolivia, and Venezuela, and then climb the Cordilleras of the spiring Andes Mountains. The bear will be easy to recognize. It will be a shaggy black animal with a yellow ring around its eyes. It will have only thirteen ribs like a dog, one less than other bears, and the spectacled bear, *Ursus ornatus,* will be the only wild species of bears one will see in all of South America.

Far away on the other side of the globe lives another small bear that also likes to climb high mountains. It is a fearsome little terror with no proper respect for people or their possessions. Charges against it include raiding orchards, tipping over beehives, mauling humans, and eating children. There is almost no rest from its depredations because it works all through the night, and prowls all winter when other bears are hibernating.

The Tibetan black bear, *Ursus thibetanus,* though it seldom attains a weight of 200 pounds, is possessed of giant strength, and has almost no fear of people. It is jet black in color, with now and then a brownish or, rarely, an albino color mutation. The hair is long and thick with a woolly undercoat that keeps it comfortably warm at 15,000 feet high in the Himalayan snow. The farmers of Kashmir, Central China, and the Amur regions have all felt the midnight sallies of the "moon" bear and so have more southerly people in Japan, Formosa, and Hainan. In spite of its destructiveness, the big-eared rascal is regarded by many mountain natives as a distant relative that they will neither kill nor eat.

On the other hand, the Asian sun bear of the lower elevations is a jolly little chap who likes to stuff himself with beetles, honey, and tropical fruits and rock himself to sleep in the tree tops. The Malayans call him *Bagindo nan tinggih*—"He who likes to sit high."

The shiny black coat of *Ursus malayanus,* the Malayan sun bear, is short and smooth as that of a pointer dog. There are prominent cowlick whorls on both shoulders, a mustard-colored throat patch, and a dangling two-inch tail. The sun bear stands upright more than other bears and makes a somewhat irresponsible pet if treated with kindness and large doses of honey. In the wild, however, it is a raging little demon when wounded or cornered. Preferring a balmier climate than the surly moon bear, the Malayan sun bear is found along the eastern lower Himalayas to Sze-Chwin, China, and south through Burma, Borneo, Sumatra, Celebes, and Java. No one could ever mistake this droll, runty creature walking upright like a pot-bellied dwarf for any other bear.

There is, however, nothing very amusing about the well-named sloth bear, *Ursus ursinus,* and its table manners are atrocious. Using its greatly oversize paws and long, curved claws for digging tools, the Indian sloth bear exposes a colony of termites, thrusts its long muzzle into the opening, and starts slurping termites from stump to stomach with alternate snorting and sucking sounds that can be heard a hundred yards away over every other sound of the jungle.

Sometimes called the Aswail, or Bhalu, the sloth bear is definitely unhandsome. It has a broad, flat nose, an ugly gray naked face, and a dingy yellow breast patch. Its ungainly body is covered with long black hair with a sort of topknot between the ears and a hump on its back. It shambles along through the humid forest in the apparent belief that it is really an ant-eater. But it is not to be trifled with. In India and Ceylon where it is the commonest of bears, the natives give the sloth bear a wide berth when they hear its vacuum cleaner operating on a termite's nest.

The showpiece of any zoo lucky enough to have one on exhibit is the panda, once believed to be a rare kind of giant raccoon but now nudged toward the bear side of the fauna. It is a striking animal boldly sectioned off in black and white. Head, neck, and saddle are pure white. Each eye is wrapped around with black; the ears are also black and so are all its legs, shoulders, undersides, and rump. The clown make-up gives the panda a comic aspect in no way justified by the perilous position it holds among living things, because it teeters on the edge of extinction.

There are two kinds of these ultra-rare, pudgy-appearing beasts. The giant panda, *Ailuropoda melanoleucus,* believed to attain the size of a grizzly bear, is said to live—if it lives at all—in an isolated part of the Hsi-fan Mountains deep in the Yen-chin and Lololand region of China. It has retreated about as far as it can go into subtropical jungles where it chomps monotonously for all the days of its life on a diet of bamboo shoots. Between times it swims in the wild rivers, climbs trees, and loafs in the sun until it is time to start chomping on more bamboo shoots.

A smaller panda, *A. fulgens,* which once trundled more extensively along the Himalaya Mountains, is now said to be confined to an ever-narrowing space in the Darjeeling-Nepal region, sometimes in deep snows at great heights. It is doubtful if either of these showy, harmless creatures will survive to the end of this century.

⁋ The Snow Bear

It was on a dog team trip along the Arctic coast in the early 1920's that I met Pooshuk, the bravest of hunters. I stumbled onto his igloo just as a violent storm came roaring in off the Chukchi Sea, and for several days he let me share his igloo while over its thick, sodded roof the blizzard shrieked with demoniac fury.

Every morning Pooshuk and I would crawl on hands and knees up a tunnel past curled-up sled dogs, break a fresh hole through the accumulating drifts, and take another look at the Niagara of snow cascading down upon us. Each time we would retreat to our underground hovel and hunker alongside the flickering seal-oil lamp. With nothing to do for another day, host Pooshuk felt called upon to provide some form of entertainment. With his crude tools he carved delicate figures on a walrus tusk. Laying the work aside, he sang the rare old Eskimo songs of his forefathers, his big voice filling the smoke-filled igloo. But mostly, Pooshuk talked about Nanook, the polar bear.

With no trace of braggadocio because it is not in the nature of the Innuit man to boast, Pooshuk told me tales that he himself had heard as he sat at the feet of his father, and as his father and other fathers before him had heard for countless generations. Of all the wild creatures of the Arctic snow and ice, the polar bear played the strongest part in Eskimo legends. A strange kind of reverence marked Pooshuk's feelings toward it. The skull of every polar bear slain by Pooshuk or his people must be placed on a high rock facing north so that its spirit might escape to find home in a white bear yet unborn. So the old Eskimo hunters, explained Pooshuk solemnly, never really destroyed Nanook, but only helped speed his soul to another and younger body.

With this belief to guide them, neither Pooshuk nor his ancestors had felt any qualms about hunting the snow bear. Each one they killed was a department store of light, heat, clothing, bedding, tools, medicine; and the rich, red meat imbued all those who ate it with the courage of Nanook. The hunter who killed a polar bear became the village hero, because every part of the animal was shared equally with the neighbors so that all might be brave and strong.

A few days before I came dogmushing along to find shelter in his igloo, Pooshuk had suffered an unexpected loss at the hands of Nanook. A bloated walrus carcass washed up on the beach sands had drawn a number of beautifully-furred Arctic foxes to the feast. Pooshuk had ringed the site with small steel traps to harvest the delicately soft furs worth $40 apiece at the trading post. Shortly afterward, calamity had struck. A gaunt polar bear had come padding off the sea ice to share in the feast. One after another, Pooshuk's precious steel traps had snapped shut on its toenails and had been wrenched loose from their fastenings. Pooshuk got there just in time to see Nanook stalking indignantly away, his feet festooned with traps and dangling chains.

Pooshuk's people had observed, long before our own biologists discovered the same trait, that except for the females coming to the windrows of jumbled ice at shoreline at cubbing time, the polar bear preferred the pelagic life. It has been found to range completely around the frozen oceans of the North frigid zone. There are no polar bears in the Antarctic. There is but one species in the Arctic. Its principal home is a floating pan of ice drifting continuously in a set pattern. For example, the polar bear on a slab of ice broken off Ellesmere Land would in eight or ten years be carried west from Greenland past Point Barrow, then be caught up in a current that takes it to the North Pole before swinging east and south again to complete the circle at Ellesmere Land, and off again on the next orbit. A separate ocean current might carry another ice pack from Siberia eastward across the Arctic Ocean past North America, Iceland, Spitzbergen, and over the top of Asia. Thus, Nanook belongs to no one country. His magic carpet of ice floats him over the wildest wastes in the Northern hemisphere, from which he may disembark at his pleasure to set foot on Alaska, Canada, Greenland, Iceland, Scandinavia, and the Soviet Union. No other four-footed animal in all the world travels so far in its lifetime.

Its home on the ice-covered ocean is by no means the biological vacuum one might surmise. It is, on the contrary, an amazingly well-stocked refrigerator. Food is plentiful, often in teeming abundance. At the bottom of the cold seas are clams, crabs and swarming clouds of pink shrimp. The ocean surface is awash with plankton that attracts whales from the seven seas. Fishes, waterfowl, foxes, and seals are noted for their fat condition in the Arctic. It is a good life, and if ever a predator seems born to thrive on the eternal ice, it is Nanook.

Yet, the polar bear was once a land mammal. It descended from the common parent of other existing bears, *Ursus arctos,* the European Brown Bear. It is now rated as a form of grizzly reshaped and decolored by environment. In the National Zoo at Washington, D.C., the close kinship between the two bears, grizzly and polar, has not only been shown by interbreeding, but the crosses have also been fertile and in turn have produced numerous offspring with various blendings of grizzly and snow bear features. Some are pure white, some silver-blue, some roan, and others grizzly brown. Some have the big head and hump of the grizzly; others the snake-like neck and narrower head of the polar bear. They are all big, healthy and rambunctious.

In sheer bulk there is not much to choose between the two giant bears, each sharing honors as the mightiest predator walking the earth today. Several polar bears have been catalogued at between 1500 and 1600 pounds—an awesome monster, indeed, to an Eskimo paddling his kayak when the great creature suddenly submerges like an iceberg awash in the water, with only its black nose tip and eyes above the surface. In such a stealthy manner Nanook approaches a seal napping on the edge of a floe, and while yet some distance away sinks entirely out of sight. Seconds later the polar bear comes rearing out of the sea alongside the seal and bashes in its head with a blow of its heavy paw.

Among the rations Pooshuk had fetched into the igloo to chew on during the blizzard was such a bear paw. Other parts of the beast, together with chunks of walrus and a score or more of eider ducks were stored outside on a high-pole cache. When I lifted the bear paw it felt like a smoked ham covered with white hair. The black pad was tough as a truck tire, pockmarked and grown across with stiffish hair to provide a non-skid surface, with stout, needle-sharp nails to give it sure traction on glare ice. "Nanook run too fast," explained Pooshuk, which meant that no Eskimo could match its speed.

He poured some more foul-smelling seal oil in the shallow stone lamp and squatted close to adjust the twisted-moss wicking. I pumped up my brass primus stove to melt some snow for coffee, and the Eskimo took advantage of its sputtering blue flame to boil his bear paw. While it was cooking, Pooshuk told me how he had acquired it. He had been awakened one night by heavy thumping on the dome of his igloo. A shaft of moonlight shining down through the air-vent in the center was suddenly cut off. In the dim light of the seal-oil lamp Pooshuk saw a big paw reach down through the opening and start probing around. It was withdrawn for a moment, and then came the nose of the beast shoved down until Pooshuk and the bear stood eye to eye. Immediately afterward the polar bear began digging furiously at the thick, frozen sod. When it stopped to peer down into the igloo again its entire head was forced through the opening. "Me think better do something," said Pooshuk.

One shot from the extended muzzle of his .30-30 rifle sent a bullet into the open mouth of the bear. Pushing cautiously through the snow-plug at the tunneled outlet of the igloo, Pooshuk found the lifeless body of the white beast and proceeded thriftily to add its bulk to other items on the platform of his cache.

"Nanook fight anything when hungry," declared Pooshuk, and grinned as another example came to mind. Once while hunting bowhead whales in the crumbling June ice with brass harpoon gun, he and his oomiak crew members had seen a polar bear jump on the back of a surfacing whale, go down with it, and come up again still trying to bite a mouthful of blubber off the forty-ton behemoth.

On the far northwestern rim of Alaska where the treeless tundra comes down from the white-chiseled mountains to meet the Arctic Ocean, gale winds regularly smash the offshore ice fields into slabs and hurl them into barriers many feet high. In these icy labyrinths the female polar bear retires to give birth to her young in midwinter. For the expectant mother it is not a true hibernation, merely a deep sleep from which she awakens to administer to her new born cubs. Like the other bear species, the snow bear infants come into the world naked, blind, and unbelievably tiny. For many weeks they must huddle in the thick fur of the mother, absorbing her body heat and suckling the warm, thick milk. They are woolly white balls the size of a small dog when the mother leads them out to meet the sun which, after several months of darkness, has risen like a red ball above the Arctic horizon. Soon afterward she will convoy her babies out onto the free ice where food is plentiful and where the smell of smoke from the native villages lies far behind. Some of the cubs, if they are males, may never again set foot on dry land, but ride the vast ice islands of the polar regions for all the days of their lives.

Sailing in their big oomiaks far at sea in search of walrus herds, Pooshuk and his crews have watched female bears guiding their cubs from berg to berg. If the cubs become tired while swimming, they may crawl out on the mother's back, or hitchhike a tow by gripping the trailing rump hairs of the parent. While they are adept swimmers, fluid and graceful as seals, the great white bears are aware that the open waters of the ocean hold the one beast capable of devouring them. It is the deadly *Orca,* or killer whale, largest and most terrifying of all flesh-eating mammals still in existence. Before the crash of rifle-fire—which all wild creatures have learned to fear—shattered the white silence of the north, Nanook and his family acknowledged no other superior, not even man. When hungry, they pursued the Eskimo as fair game. Pooshuk's own father had once met such an attack with a flint-headed spear. The bear had ripped his face so badly that he lost the sight of one eye, and his left arm was mangled so as to be useless for the rest of his days. But he slew the white beast and distributed its flesh generously among his tribesmen, with extra portions for his first son Pooshuk so that he would be sure to grow up into a brave hunter.

Pooshuk says he is not sure the magic potions helped him, though his own way with a polar bear was certainly not for the faint of heart. When he went out on the ice he wore an over-garment of white drill which made him well-nigh invisible. Upon reaching a spot where the seals were hauling out to rest, Pooshuk stretched himself flat and shed his white parka to reveal the dark sealskin garments underneath. Then he began at carefully spaced intervals to kick his mukluk-clad feet in the air to simulate the flippers of a basking seal, pausing now and then to feign sleep, and occasionally raising his head the way a seal will do between naps. The smell of the oil-soaked sealskin garments no less than the dark profile on the ice was certain to attract the first prowling polar bear to cross downwind. Then would begin its belly-creeping stalk, hair-raising indeed for the intended victim imitating its favorite food.

"Make-um come close," insisted Pooshuk. "Too much close!"

There seemed to be a point about fifty feet away where the crouching bear dug in for the final rush, and that was the time to sit up quickly and pull the trigger.

In the murk of the seal-oil lamp I reached over to examine Pooshuk's bear-hunting rifle. It was a very old, many-times-repaired lever action model woefully inadequate by any standards I knew. When I tried to work its salt-corroded mechanism it required both my hands and a braced foot to jack one cartridge out of the firing chamber and force another in. With a charging bear it was strictly a one-shot affair, or likely even a misfire. I was shaking my head as I handed it back, but Pooshuk seemed to think he had enough advantage; certainly a lot more than his father ever knew.

Somewhat sadly, as if he were failing to live up to his ancestors, he said, "My father maybe not very proud for this way."

I shall forever wonder what he thought of me a few days later when the storm abated and I firmly declined his invitation to go polar bear hunting with him and lay down on the ice to make like a seal. But he let me off the hook most tactfully.

"Maybe white man no stink good," he considered carefully. "Maybe Nanook no like-um."

q More Polar Bears

So I was not doing a sleeping seal imitation when I encountered my first polar bear. I was driving a team of eleven spirited huskies across the 40-mile-wide entrance to Kotzebue from Cape Espenberg to Cape Blossom, the sled tracks behind me following almost exactly a segment of the Arctic Circle. On the map the cutoff from Cape to Cape showed one hundred fewer miles of travel than the safer trail along the shoreline, and for the first hour the frozen sea was smooth as a skating rink. The dogs were racing along in fine fettle, tails curled over their backs, heads in the air sniffing for game, when they came to a pressure ridge. Careening over its top of broken ice packed with hard-drifted snow I saw the reason why the huskies were giving me such an exhilarating, 30-below-zero ride. It was a freshly killed seal and crouched over it was a yearling polar bear.

With a savage chorus of delight the sled dogs charged straight toward the young bear, and to my surprise little 300-

pound Nanook deserted his kill and went scrambling and dodging away over the broken ice field with astonishing squirts of speed. As the sled shot by the partly-eaten seal I reached over and swung it aboard. The huskies would have it for their supper that night, but now they paid no attention. They were out for bigger game; out to bring Nanook to a stand and harass him by their numbers. But this small polar bear had no intention of facing a pack of howling huskies. They were snapping at its rump, and all the makings of a murderous melee were closing together when the bear sighted an open lead among the ice pans. Suddenly, Nanook jack-knifed at right angles, dove into the green water and vanished in a cloud of bubbles.

Three of the lead dogs skidded into the sea behind it before I could jam on the brake. I had to drag them out one at a time, knock the ice out of their harnesses and get the team headed back on course to Cape Blossom. Exciting as the chase had been, I hoped there would be no more polar bear episodes during the rest of the day's travel. But I was wrong. We hadn't traveled a dozen miles before another polar bear hove into view. This one was a full-grown adult and it was looking for trouble.

Though the big bear was yet some distance away to my side and rear, it had drawn bead on the dog team and was shuffling in off the outer ice at an angle to intercept what it probably had mistaken for other white bears. Tossing its head high to correct its line, it looked as powerful as a tractor as it flowed smoothly up and down the ice ridges toward a sideswipe with the dog team. I had no wish to shoot the beast, but it did seem to be good judgment to draw my rifle from its leather scabbard, blow the sight free of snow, and work the bolt to put a cartridge into firing position. The way I was being jounced about at the handlebars of the sled I doubt that I could have hit the broad side of an elephant.

It was at this juncture that an unexpected diversion took place. The huskies had by now sensed the tension and were trying to locate the source when an arctic fox, white and fluffy as a powder puff, flushed from under the lead dog's nose and went scampering away like a tumbleweed in the wind. The entire team took off in furious pursuit on a chase as hopeless as whippets straining for a mechanical rabbit. By the time they flopped on the ice, tongues hanging out with exhaustion, we were almost across to Cape Blossom and the polar bear was nowhere in sight.

Trader Jim Allen smiled indulgently when I told him I'd seen two polar bears in the same day. Old-timer Jim had operated a fur-trading post at Wainright for many years and was, himself, one of the greatest hunters in all of Arctic Alaska.

"Bears?" mused Big Jim. "Why, I've seen 'em thicker'n seagulls on a beach." He crammed his pipe full of plug cut, held the flame of an old-fashioned sulphur match to it, and puffed his memories into focus. "Young feller, you want to hear about polar bears?"

In the late summer of 1914 Jim Allen was returning from the "Outside," meaning the States, on the bark *Belvedere* bound for Herschel Island on the Arctic Ocean shore of Yukon Territory to "freeze in" for the winter with a load of trade goods for native bartering. They'd loitered overlong to dicker with Chukchi tribes along the Siberian coast and by the time the *Belvedere* sailed around Point Barrow to Icy Reef the polar winter was upon them. Surging ice fields pinned them to the shore line, and the only escape route was a narrow lead of shallow water between the huge grounded bergs and the beach.

Leaving a watch party aboard the ice-locked *Belvedere,* Jim Allen and a crew of seven Eskimo volunteers started back to Point Barrow, more than 500 miles away, in an open whale-boat. They'd rowed as far as Beechey Point, roughly halfway, when the lead froze into a mass of churning slush. "We had no choice," recalled Trader Jim as he sucked at his pipe. "We had to take to the beach and walk all the way to Point Barrow; we had to carry a month's supply of food or starve to death."

Ingenious Jim had bent the blades of two oars to fashion a crude sledge for hauling their bedding and supplies. They'd had to wait ten precious days for the slush ice to bear their weights, and then they'd harnessed themselves like dogs and started dragging the sledge. Jim had eked out their slimming rations by shooting seals along the way. "I had just four cartridges left," he said, "when we ran into the polar bears."

In the eerie optical illusions of the dim Arctic twilight stretching forever in all directions, color-lighted at intervals by flashing displays of Northern Lights, the off-white objects in the distance puzzled Big Jim. "They looked like seagulls gathered around a dead seal," he told me, "or maybe just another mirage."

Because they had no choice but to hold their compass course, Jim and his seven Eskimos plodded steadily toward the things barring their way to Point Barrow until they'd narrowed the distance enough to make positive identification. "The dark object was not a seal," stated Trader Jim. "It was the carcass of a huge bowhead whale foundered a quarter mile off the beach line. The white creatures were bears. We counted more than a hundred of them tearing chunks of blubber off the whale. Some were lying around on the ice sleeping off their blubber jags; some were walking along the whale's back; some others had eaten a hole into the belly of the whale big enough so they were walking inside and coming out the whale's mouth." Jim shook his head as if to clarify the scene. "It was the damndest sight you ever saw!"

Two of the bears came out to meet the sledge party, and Jim managed to put down each one with a single shot. This left the party with only two more cartridges, which Jim "figured we'd better save for an emergency." They loaded the sledge with fresh bear meat, detoured around the dead whale at a safe distance and ten days later came necking their load into Point Barrow village.

Several other times in his far north adventures, Jim Allen had found what he called "herds" of polar bears gathered around defunct whales, drawn to the feast from incredibly far distances. He didn't think any other animal in the world had such a keen, choke-bored nose, and had seen enough examples to convince him that a polar bear could smell a decaying whale for more than twenty miles.

The white fox my dog team had routed near the polar bear was no surprise to Jim Allen. "Nanook's little helpers," he nodded. "They often run together. Next time you see a polar bear out on the ice, look carefully and you'll like as not spot an arctic fox or two hanging around to pick up the bear's leavings. They'll scout ahead as lookouts and somehow contrive to let the bear know when they've found something to interest a big guy like him."

Such game might be a pod of walrus hauled out on a floating berg, looking like gigantic brown slugs with their armorplate wrinkled hides. Groaning and snoring in their sleep, their vision blurry and myopic, they are easy to stalk from down wind. But killing one is something else. If the pod contains a few old bulls with two-foot-long ivory tusks, Nanook will usually leave the two-ton slumberer strictly alone. Rarely, when goaded by desperate hunger, the white bear will take a chance. Once Jim came upon the scene of such a combat. The ice was red with blood. The walrus was gone. The polar bear, wallowing in its gore, was punched full of holes and quite dead.

When the snow bear can choose its own way to dine on walrus flesh, it will crouch at the ice edge to wait for a young one to come swimming along close enough to be knocked stiff with a blow from a ham-sized paw. The white bear will wait for hours at a seal's breathing hole to deliver the same kind of a knockout.

Only when the pickings are lean will the polar bear fill his
empty paunch with ducks. To catch the fat eiders as they float
on the frigid sea, Nanook goes into his disappearing act, sinking below the waves until only three black spots are visible: a
nose and two sharp eyes. The first warning the eiders usually
get is when one of their number is mysteriously jerked out of
sight. If they try to escape by diving, Nanook spins down upon
them like an otter pursuing a fish. "Nobody will believe this
if you write it," cautioned Jim, "but I have also seen a polar
bear grubbing grass on the edge of the tundra."

With his natural talents as an observer, backed by a good
library of outdoor books which he pored over during the long
winter nights, Big Jim Allen was a storehouse of information
about wildlife in the Arctic. His specialty was the polar bear,
and he was forever prying into their secrets. He'd seen the
females being courted in early summer. With the coming of
winter when the sun went down to rise no more for many
weeks, he'd seen their tracks leading to dens in the jumbled
ice barriers, and rarely into the mountains beyond the tundra.
He knew that the newborn cubs were so small he could hold
three of them in the palm of his hand. He knew that like their
grizzly cousins, the polar bear female is a doting mother and
will not again encourage a lover until her cubs are through
nursing and are big enough to fend for themselves. This would
mean two years between matings, which are sometimes promiscuous affairs involving several boars.

Year after year the Eskimos brought squalling polar bear
cubs to Jim Allen's fur station to be hand reared by Big Jim
until they sailed away on trading schooners to zoo homes all
over the country. Jim knew polar bears as few men will, and
he was concerned about their future in a fast-changing world.
He was especially worried over the coming of small ski-
equipped airplanes to the Arctic; of their ability to take man
where no man had ever been before, to far places that for the
white bears had once been a haven of space. Several years

after my visits with Jim Allen and shortly before he passed away, he wrote me: "There's no place for Nanook to hide any more."

He didn't live to see the plane-hunting of polar bears become an established business in the far north. In his own day a hunt for the great snow bear involved several dog teams, the most noted of Eskimo hunters, special native fur clothing, and camping on the ice fields in subzero storms. It was adventure! It was exploration, and the trophy attained was a treasure beyond price. Jim wasn't around to see the hunters arrive from the States by air during the long daylight of spring; to ride in warmed cabins of chartered planes far out over the frozen ocean, with another pilot flying escort in case of accident. The shooting was comparatively easy. The great beasts showed little fear when the gasoline bird lighted on the ice alongside and the hunter stepped out to shoot. The element of risk was in the flying itself and the landings and takeoffs in rough ice and frequent stormy conditions.

The young, daredevil pilots wouldn't have had to give Jim Allen their best argument in favor of plane-hunting: that it took them far from land to where the biggest polar bears are found, and that their kills were mostly huge males in international ice fields. Jim would know all this. What he wouldn't abide was the total lack of sportsmanship involved, the shooting down of a beast that had no chance to defend itself or run away.

Possibly, the white bear may learn some day to recognize the chatter of an airplane as a deadly sound, as the timber wolf has learned, and will flee into the protection of upended ice slabs or take other evasive action. But they still have much to find out. Bernt Balchen, the famous Norwegian-American pilot who flew over both poles and helped teach Canadians the art of bush-flying in winter, once told me of a forced landing on the ice of Hudson Bay. Early next morning while he lay in his sleeping bag, Bernt was awakened by the lurching of his plane. He opened the door to see a huge polar bear scratching its back against the rear stabilizer.

Our Armed Forces in Greenland and other far north stations during the last war found the big snow bears almost as innocent. The evidence is clear that they are among the least suspicious of all bears, the most vulnerable to modern hunting methods. As they ride the polar merry-go-round of drifting ice, past several nations that abut the Arctic ice fields, the white bears are subject to conflicting regulations, or to none at all.

Trader Jim Allen once called Nanook "the bear without a country," and suggested that it should, some day, be included in International Treaties already set up for whales, walrus, seals, and other pelagic creatures. Why not now?

q The Black Jaspers of Anan

When "D Boone kilt a bar" in the Kentucky woodlands back in the 1740's it was a black bear species. Two hundred years later when .30-40 Joe shot and missed one at Anan Creek in Southeastern Alaska it was also a black bear. And if Daniel Boone were still around, .30-40 Joe would be glad to argue the point on who had the better reason to do the shooting. "I claim it was me," declared the old Alaska homesteader stoutly. "No bear could be so ornery as the black jasper that broke into my cabin."

Joe is, so he says, a man of considerable patience. Living his hermit life at the mouth of Anan Creek where as many as a hundred black bears congregate each summer to catch the spawning salmon, the old settler has learned to put up with a reasonable amount of bear mischief. He tolerates their robbing of his huckleberry patch alongside his cabin. They can even flatten his vegetable garden and stand on their hind feet to peer through his windows at night. "I'm neighbor to the bears because I like 'em a lot better'n I do most people," he declares firmly. "But that doesn't mean I can't be pushed too far by 'em."

The incident rankles anew in .30-40 Joe's mind as he recalls what happened. He'd tramped down to the beach to dig a bucket of butter clams for his dinner, and when he got back to his cabin the door was wide open. His furniture had been rearranged. The table had been tipped over, his chair up-ended, pots and pans scattered around the floor, but only one item was missing. When .30-40 Joe discovered what it was, he could scarcely believe his eyes. It was a keg of salt salmon!

"There was a million fresh salmon in the creek waiting for the bears to pick 'em up," said Joe indignantly. "But no, that black jasper wanted mine!"

He snatched his rifle off its pegs and started looking for the lost keg. When he caught up with it, it had been rolled half way down the hill toward the creek. "The lid was stove in, and my salt salmon sides were spilling out. And when the bear seen me it fetched the keg another clout. That," said .30-40 Joe, "is when I parted its hair in the middle with a rifle ball."

Up and down this continent from Alaska to Florida and from the Maritime Provinces of Canada to California, the black bear has inspired more zany tales than any other big-game animal. Depending on how it treats its human neighbors, it is amusing, destructive, pestiferous, sometimes even dangerous. No other bear has shown such uncanny ability to survive in the midst of those who would gun it down. Today, in spite of telescope-sighted rifles and upwards of twenty million nimrods combing America's woodlands, the black bear population within the United States remains surprisingly high. There are uncountable thousands north to the tree limit in Canada and in the baking-hot hills of old Mexico. They live high in the snow-capped mountains of the West. They wallow in the cane-brakes of Louisiana's tepid, sea-level swamps. They catch fish in Yukon's waters, kill moose calves in British Columbia, steal pigs in Georgia, rob beehives in Michigan, and cadge handouts from tourists in our National Parks.

The black bear is many things to many people. Under its glossy coat waddles villain, thief, jester, and above all a creature very determined to live.

"Come on down to the creek with me," invited .30-40 Joe. "I'll show you a little feller who don't know how to quit."

The old homesteader led me along a trail through the big evergreens along the edge of Anan Creek where he sometimes served as summer stream watchman to prevent poachers from seining the massed hordes and delivering them to the salmon canneries. The annual run was hitting its peak. The shallow riffles, in places no more than six inches deep, were solidly jammed with humpbacked salmon depositing their roe and milt. Dying and dead spawned-out salmon were drifting slowly back toward salt water. Others surging in from the sea were jumping the falls to reach less crowded gravel beds upstream. Hundreds of thousands more were finning at the surface of the bay just off the river mouth waiting their turn to get in.

Under a canopy of fluttering gulls and circling ravens, the bears were glutting themselves with salmon. Some of them had already gorged until their bellies hung pendulous and were sprawled along the banks sleeping. Young ones no bigger than cocker spaniels were tearing up and down the pools wrestling, bickering, playing tag, and splashing water on one another, paying almost no attention to .30-40 Joe whom they saw every day as he made his rounds. A big, jet-black boar that must have weighed 500 pounds was bedded down across the trail. It groaned, blew foam from its lips, and bristled its neck hairs at us; and we honored the bluff by taking another trail around it. For the summering bears on Anan Creek life was beautiful. There was only one exception.

It was a small bear, a runt that through fighting with another bear or being struck with a rifle bullet, had lost its entire lower jaw. "He should be dead," commented .30-40 Joe. "But look at him!"

The little under-privileged bear had herded a salmon into a shallow cul-de-sac and crushed out its life by falling on it with the full weight of his chest. With his sharp foreclaws he then proceeded to rake strips of pink flesh off the bones and poke them into his throat like tamping charges down the muzzle of a cap and ball musket.

If .30-40 Joe had a favorite character among the bears of Anan Creek, this snipe-nosed yearling was the one. But he knew when to draw the line on bear pets. He'd seen what happened to a neighbor living thirty miles down the bay shore who picked up a kitten-sized cub and bottle-fed it to weaning age. By this time the little she cub, which he called Matilda, had come to believe the neighbor was her mother and refused to join the wild ones. She liked his cooking a lot better than raw salmon out of the creeks and stowed away prodigious stacks of flapjacks sopped in syrup.

Finally, in November, the neighbor reported to .30-40 Joe that Matilda had failed to show up for breakfast. There wasn't a sign of her all winter. But one morning in May when he was frying flapjacks he heard something stirring under the floor. The next minute a black bear walked into the cabin, sat up on its haunches and began waving paws in the air. It was Matilda. She'd hibernated under the cabin all winter, and now she was all set again for another summer as star boarder.

"It wasn't the same any more," lamented the neighbor. "Matilda was too big now. She'd outlived her welcome. She was still playful as all get out; always sitting up trying to coax me into a sparring match like when she was a little cub. But when she belted me now it was like being kicked by a mule with claws on its hoofs."

The neighbor, concluded .30-40 Joe, enticed his overgrown pet into his gas boat with a platter of flapjacks and turned her

loose on a salmon stream a hundred miles down the coast. He
hopes he's seen the last of her, but he isn't sure. Every time a
black bear shows up in the clearing near his cabin he thinks
it's Matilda come back to eat him out of house and home.

Walking the banks of a river where a hundred or more wild
black bears spend their summers has given hermit Joe first
hand knowledge of their family affairs. He notes that the
young, first-time mothers seldom have more than a single cub.
Only the older females, which he has learned to recognize year
after year, produce twins, triplets, or rarely quintuplets. He
also had a logical theory why the infants weigh only six or
seven ounces and are so extremely tiny in proportion to the
size of the parent. Born in midwinter while the mother is asleep
in her den and must live for many weeks on her own fat, the
smaller the cubs the less drain on the mother. This is also the
reason why the first bears out of hibernation in the spring are
the females with cubs, and the last ones to show are the hog-
fat old boars.

The mother knows it will be a couple of months before the
salmon run is due and she fills out the time and her belly with
tender shoots of marsh grass, roots, carrion, bugs and crabs
along the tide flats, and happiest adventure of all, by raiding
campsites and deserted log cabins. Mostly, the cubs romp
ahead of mama bear, all ears and quivering noses and beady
black eyes, plus a boundless capacity for getting into scrapes.

"They can't wait to get into trouble," said .30-40 Joe. "I
watched one little feller stick a paw into the open shells of a
big clam and they pinched shut on him like a mouse trap. He
went bouncing all over the mud flats, flinging his paw around
and squalling bloody murder." Joe grinned at the recollection.
"The mother just sat back on her haunches, mouth open like
she was laughing, and let the little feller work loose by himself. I guess she figured he'd be into a lot of worse messes than

that before he grew up, and he might as well start learning how to take care of himself."

Black bears share with other bears an inborn fear of dogs sometimes ridiculously out of balance with the situation. Homesteader Joe had seen such an instance on Anan Creek. "Feller walked up the river bank here one day with a yapping fox terrier and filled the trees full of bears."

Of course the bears knew that a feisty, pint-sized mutt weighing less than a dozen pounds couldn't hurt them. They were just responding to a primitive urge of ages past when packs of fierce, giant wolves swept through the forests attacking and devouring almost any creature that stood in their path. But to .30-40 Joe it was downright humiliating to see his beloved bears routed by a lap dog. The climax came when the same giant old boar that bluffed Joe and me off the trail with its teeth-chomping routine, took one look at the little dog and lumbered hastily into the tall timbers. The man started bragging about his dog and it was too much for .30-40 Joe to endure. The peace and tranquility of Anan Creek were at stake.

Said Joe, "I told the feller to take his little bully off the creek and never bring it back."

❡ Black Mischief

The black bears would all be enjoying better reputations if they had tables set with salmon and huckleberries like the summer menu at .30-40 Joe's Anan Creek in Southeastern Alaska. But the harsh fact is that their original range in America is being taken over by human settlers at a terrifying rate. Their natural way of life is being trimmed away until many of the bears must steal from the farmers or starve. In British Columbia where small ranches are rapidly displacing yesterday's wilderness sanctuaries, the black bear is by no means a welcome sight.

"One of the bloody beggars killed eighteen of my sheep in one night," an irate stockman told me. "It was a young bear, at that. I could tell by the way it attacked the sheep."

The pastured animals had been gashed on the flanks and rump, the mark of a black bear that hadn't learned how to kill quickly. The older bears always went for the front end, pulling the head to one side and sinking their teeth into the base of the neck. Before the sheep were placed in view of the black bears to tempt them, the bears had thrived in the same area by digging out rodents, tearing apart stumps for grubs and termites, and raiding ant hills. After batting the top off an anthill, the bear would sit on its haunches with one paw resting in the fractured entrance until it was covered with ants. Then, with one lick of the paw it would slurp the spicy mites down and reset the trap over and over again. With its claws spread apart the bear carded wild berries from the bushes with astonishing celerity. It rolled over boulders to get at the crickets and mice, and when it found a wild bee's nest it devoured honey, wax, larva bees and all, unmindful of the stings.

While always on the watch to waylay deer, elk, and calf moose, the black bear's total effect was not considered very serious. It was only when bruin got its first taste of domestic stock, usually from a dead carcass, that it learned to stalk and kill for itself. Once it became a killer of farm animals, the Canadians have found but one sure way to break the habit.

Down in the Olympic forests of Washington State the black bears have aroused the wrath of tree farmers by peeling the sticky-sweet cambium bark layer from second growth Douglas firs. Says Bear Bill Hulet, whose job it is to hold down damage, "I've knowed a single b'ar to wreck five hundred firs in a season."

Bear Bill, a Paul Bunyan character who claims he was "born under a stump, suckled on sow-b'ar milk, and raised in jail," has been pursuing black bears for most of his life. Out on the Olympic Peninsula, where the jip-loggers all know Bill Hulet, he is acclaimed the champ bear hunter of Washington State and maybe of the rest of the world. Ever since he came to grips with his first black bear at the age of 12, hefty Bill has been combing the cutoffs with a pack of hounds, a brush rifle, and a pair of calk-soled logger's boots. Weighted with 240 pounds of rubber-thewed man, these spiked boot soles have been tearing chips out of stumps and windfalls for forty years, come forest fire hell or high water.

He lets you know there is no thought of wiping out the

black rascals, just pruning off enough to save the new timber crop. Even with Bill's daily toll, black bears of the big tree country show little sign of decline. The Alaska Department of Fish and Game says that in the moss-hung rain forests where Hulet and his hounds prowl the skid roads, the bears are excessive and therefore rated as "predators" with no closed season or bag limit. Because the bear's flesh in Washington is highly odoriferous from a mixed diet of resinous pitch and spawned out salmon, and because a man needs calked shoes and the constitution of a "timber beast" to get around in the old logging slashes, practically nobody goes after them except the old pro, Bear Bill Hulet.

"It's an uphill job," sighed Bill, sizing me up narrowly as I rode with him on his "varmint" patrol. "I could use me a helper."

He flung open the back of his 4-wheel-drive rig and out jumped Bozo, King, Spot, Rock, and Red. Bill bellowed affectionately at his "pot-lickers" and beckoned to me. Then he clamped down hard on a dead cigar butt and went charging into a cascara thicket. I found myself hurdling after him over a barbed wire entanglement of blackberry briars and managed to catch up for a moment as he stopped to take his bearings. He was listening intently. His unlighted butt, mashed like a paintbrush between clenched teeth, suddenly froze at a 45-degree angle as Bozo's squeal drifted up from a tangled man-trap of downed trees, salal vine, giant ferns, and beaver dams. There was a period of dead silence like when a fuse is burning close to the powder keg, then came an explosion from the hounds. Said Bill, "Let's go git him. They've treed."

In the eleven western states' lands where huge parcels of public domain like national forests, national parks, and Bureau of Reclamation are available to them the black bears still have plenty of space to roam without having to face a rifle-toting farmer every time they come out in the open. But in the eastern half of the nation where 97 to 99 percent of the lands are cut up into private holdings, the bear is forced to hide in thickets and swamps, venturing out only at nightfall. If there are natural foods available—grubs, berries, and roots —bruin will seldom molest its human neighbors. But if food is scarce and it strays into the clearings to do what—to a citizen of the bear family—comes natural, like tearing the limbs off fruit trees, wallowing through fields of standing grain, satisfying a sweet tooth with an assault on the farmer's beehives, or stealing one of his squealing shoats, great is the hue and cry against the black bandit. Wherever one of the shaggy, low-slung, somehow menacing beasts is sighted the verdict is "guilty!"

With its sensitive nostrils questing the breeze for carrion— a winter-killed elk in Wyoming, a cow that sickened and died in Wisconsin, a stillborn colt in Montana, a flock of sheep ravaged by loose dogs in Vermont—the bear moves in to do a job of scavenging and gets tagged for the murder rap.

Even so, the black bear has growing numbers of friends, a lot of them in the places where it counts most. A game commissioner from Michigan spoke for the majority of his associates when he summed it up this way: "Sure, the black bear is a mischief-maker. Sure, it's always stirring up trouble somewhere. Sure, it does a lot of damage. But it is also a tremendous outdoor attraction, and the public wants us to save it."

Because of its low breeding potential, the black bear can never get out of bounds. The female's first cub will not arrive until she is three years of age. There will not be another until she is five. In the same period a doe deer, by way of contrast, would have an expectancy of six fawns.

As tallied by the U.S. Fish and Wildlife Service in 1960 with figures supplied by the individual states, the national score card on black bears shows a somewhat surprising current population upwards of 200,000. Nearly a third of them are in the four Pacific coastal states of Alaska, where there are

75,000. Washington has 25,000; Oregon, 20,000; California, 20,000. Montana, Idaho, Wyoming, and Colorado in the Rocky Mountain region also have goodly, though unestimated, numbers.

In the central and eastern half of the country North Carolina leads the bruin parade with 10,000, closely followed by Minnesota, Wisconsin, and Maine. The latest count for the state of New York showed an amazing 4,000. Vermont came next with 3,500, New Mexico with 3,000, Arizona with 1,600. Pennsylvania, noted for its herd of almost 400,000 white-tailed deer, somehow managed to harbor about 1,300 black bears, roughly one for every three hundred deer. Michigan is down to 1,190 black bears.

States with less than a thousand bears still roaming at large included New Hampshire and Florida with 800 each, Georgia and West Virginia with 500 each. Alabama claims a precise figure of 266. Tennessee says it has 250, and Utah's count is 200. Down to less than a hundred bruins each are South Carolina, New Jersey, Missouri, Mississippi, Texas, and Nevada. And the following states could no longer produce a single black bear in a door-to-door census: Kansas, Nebraska, North and South Dakota, Oklahoma, Connecticut, Delaware, Illinois, Indiana, Iowa, Rhode Island and, of course, Hawaii, which never did have any.

Belated appreciation of the black bear's human-interest value has done away with bounties once paid for its scalp. The six states of Nevada, Texas, Alabama, Mississippi, Missouri, and Arkansas—sharing a total of less than 400 bears—have gone all the way by granting their surviving black bears a year-round closed season. All the other states have bestowed the status of a desirable game animal on the once maligned black bear, with carefully regulated open and closed shooting seasons and bag limits. So, except for some of the rare color phases like the blue glacier bear of Southeastern Alaska and the white Kermode bear of British Columbia's islands,

Ursus americanus will far outlive our other two bear species, the polar and the grizzy. Only California and Minnesota reported a decline in the past ten years. Alabama, Pennsylvania, and Vermont even reported more bears!

Across the length of Canada there are fully as many black bears, doubtless more, than in all of the United States. South of our border Mexico has a sparse but persistent population in the northern one-fifth of the country of what they call *Oso negro*, though it is completely absent from the lower two-thirds where the jungle takes over. It likes the pine oak forests of Sierra Madre Occidental as far down as Zacatecas, and the upper part of Sonora to the American border. Oso's diet of madrone berries and acorns makes the flesh highly edible to the Mexicans, and for the choicest of all cooking oils the rendered bear fat is *mucho gusto*!

As a result, the bear is a favorite object of the chase down Mexico way. A vaquero, adept with the lariat, told me that he once tried to rope a bear out of a tree with surprising results.

"One moment, *señor*, I am on the groun' poolin' the bear from the tree. Then the bear, hees jomp from the other side from the tree weeth the rope aroun' hees neck, and then I am the one een the tree and the bear ees on the groun' tryin' to pool me down with heem." The vaquero lifted his arms to attest the truth of his tale. "Believe me, señor, eet ees only then I theenk to let go from the rope." Sadly, the vaquero concluded the story of his bear hunt. "That bear weeth my rope aroun' hees neck ees goin' somewhere yet, I theenk."

Back across the border in Georgia's mysterious Okefenokee Swamp, Manager Edwards had his own experience with a bear in a tree. He was balanced precariously in the narrow bow of a tippy native pirogue holding a camera while a taciturn, hawk-eyed character named Jess poled him silently through a lily-padded fairyland of reflections from a cypress forest draped with swaying moss. After a while Jess pointed to a big black bear well up in an overhanging bay tree feasting on wild grapes. Totally absorbed, the bear paid no attention while the guide poled noiselessly until they were underneath the tree. Suddenly, Jess cut loose with a savage scream. Instantly, the bear let go all holds and fell *kerwhump* into the swamp alongside, dousing Edwards in a geyser of tea-colored water and almost flipping the pirogue upside down.

Jess waited until the bear had floundered ashore, crashed out of sound in the bushes, and silence had once more descended on the swamp. Then he spoke. "They'll do it every time."

With the coming of night the utter darkness of Okefenokee echoes with a spine-tingling potpourri of sounds. Above the tremulous twitterings of small creatures is the hooting of owls, the startling shriek of herons, the din of a million bullfrogs, the hoarse roars of bull alligators, and the sudden caterwaul of a panther.

On such a night Manager Edwards and a patrolman waited in a hidden cabin where they had found signs of a poacher coming to skin his illegal catch of alligators before slipping out of the refuge in the morning. In the midnight hours they heard paddling outside. "He's coming," whispered the patrolman, loosening his holster. With finger on the switch, Edwards swung a searchlight to face the door. The paddling stopped and presently soft steps neared the cabin and a shadow blacker than the night filled the open doorway.

The patrolman nudged Edwards. "Now!" he hissed.

In the blinding searchlight beams was a poacher, though not a man. "It was," declared Manager Edwards, "Old Mose, the biggest black bear in the swamp!"

Dazed by the glare, Mose plunged back into the water, swam to a nearby island, and added his own angry snorts to the Okefenokee night chorus.

The protection of National Wildlife Refuges like Georgia's Okefenokee Swamp quickly becomes known to the sagacious black bears. "If caught poaching outside the swamp," said

Manager Edwards, "they scuttle full tilt for the boundary line and let me try to make peace with the angry farmers while they swagger around inside as if they owned the place."

Anyone who has been held up by the black bear bandits of our National Parks can see for himself how completely they can change their attitude towards humans. Here in their sanctuary, man is no longer the carrier of a smoke-stick from whom they must flee in terror, but a harmless soft-touch to be waylaid at every parking place. Yellowstone with 500 of such moochers; Grand Teton and Glacier Parks with 200 each; Great Smokies' with 140, and the other National and State Parks and Wildlife Refuges spaced across the land, are all free hotels to the black bears. And they know it!

꧁ The Black Bear's Way of Life

During the Klondike gold rush, miners' tents blossomed like daisies along the creek banks, and while the prospectors were striking gold, the black bears were discovering a delicious new line of food. Sacks of flour and sugar, dried fruits, smoked meats—staple grub of the sourdoughs—were theirs for the stealing. Quickly overcoming their natural fear of man, the bears of the Klondike became artful pilferers, plundering the camps while the miners were away working their claims, and sometimes creeping among the sleeping men at night to help themselves.

Frank Kelley, a son of Ireland who toiled up over the Dyea Trail to reach the Dawson diggings in 1897, told me that a group of prospectors in a gulch above Discovery Creek almost came to a shooting war with one another before they discovered the real culprit among them.

"The situation became so bad," declares Kelley, "that I not only cut initials on me last slab of bacon, but took it to bed and slept with it under me pillow." The old Irish pioneer shakes his head sadly. "A divil bit of good it did me. Whin I woke up one morning it was gone."

Kelley, never the lad to avoid a melee in his younger years, charged from one tent to another examining bacon slabs. Failing to come up with a winner, he then checked on the camp sled dogs. They were all properly chained to their stakes. Acting on a hunch, he turned four of them loose and soon they were howling fiercely at the foot of a scrub spruce. The miners all gathered to unmask the villain. Peering down through the branches at them with the guilty look of a small boy caught with his fingers in the jam pot was a yearling black bear.

Says Kelley, "There wasn't a man among us mean enough to shoot the little divil."

Instead, they all agreed to adopt the black imp as camp mascot, and collected enough scraps to keep it reasonably honest. The kind deed brought him luck, claims Kelley, and that fall he headed down the Yukon River with a poke-full of Klondike nuggets in a whip-sawed boat. But at Fort St. Michael on the Bering Sea, where he planned to sail for the "Great Outside," it took another bear to recharge his luck.

The only ocean-going vessel left in the wind-scourged port, the last ship of the season to go south, was a derelict old coal-burner with the proud name of *Discoverer*. Her slimy planking was sieved with teredo holes, Kelley says, her masts were dry-rotted and her staterooms smelled of bilge water and worse. To bolster his courage before going aboard for the 2,000-mile voyage to Seattle, Kelley swigged a bottle of rum at the local trading post.

"As long as the good Lord lets me live," declares Kelley, hale and hearty in his middle 80's, "I'll be grateful for the bear that stood in me way that day."

On the narrow boardwalk to the dock, Kelley had to pass the military post where the soldiers had a black bear chained alongside the path. Unknown to Kelley, the soldiers had tor-

mented the creature until it was touchier than a poked rattle-
snake. When the daring son of the Auld Sod came reeling by,
the bear reared up on its hind feet, hung out its lower jaw in a
defiant gesture, and moaned a dare as it struck a boxer's stance
with its front paws. This was too much for a fighting man by
the name of Kelley.

"Spittin' on me hands," he recalls, "I danced in with me left
ready to play a stiff-arm tattoo on the beast's ugly snout; me
right fist cocked to be buried in its soft potbelly."

To this day, close to seventy years later, Kelley cannot remember what happened after he fired his left jab. All he
knows is that a passing soldier picked him up off the tundra
thirty feet away and dragged him back to the bunkhouse.

"Whin I woke up two days later," says Kelley, "me neck
felt like it had been jerked loose, and there was a knot on me
head the size of a goose egg."

Staggering blurry-eyed to the nearest window he peered out
at the Bering Sea roadstead. There was nothing but cold gray
water as far as he could see. The *Discoverer* had sailed for the
Outside. Kelley was still bemoaning his bad luck several days
later when a radio message crackled into the Army cable station. The *Discoverer* had broken apart in a storm and gone to
the bottom. The only survivor on its passenger list was Kelley.

Though the black bear is not generally regarded as a dangerous wild beast, there is no questioning its ability to kill a
human as quickly as can its grizzly cousin. It reaches a top
weight of 600 pounds which is, in fact, heavier than many
grizzlies, and in its dark brown and cinnamon color phases
often occurring in litters of blacks, it has sometimes been mistaken for the grizzly. The difference, of course, is pronounced.
The black bear has a smaller, narrower head which it holds
higher as it trudges along. It also lacks the grizzly's shoulder
hump. Its claws are shorter, more curved, and very sharp for
climbing trees. In the wild the black bear does a remarkable

job of avoiding man, fleeing at the first taint of human scent. It is only when wounded, cornered, or its cubs are in danger that the black bear sometimes attacks and maims people. No big-game animal or domestic stock can withstand its assault, and the only wonder is that its depredations are not more frequent or severe.

The answer probably lies in the observation that the black bear does not have the habitually sour disposition of its grizzly kin. It is inclined to be friendly—as friendly as hunters will permit—though maintaining a watchful suspicion of all humans. If it could have its own way it would undoubtedly prefer the seclusion of primitive forests where it once filled its belly with natural easy-to-come-by bounties of the land, like wild fruits, roots, fish, bugs, and rodents. But this way of life is having to give way to closer contact with people, and it can bring embarrassing moments to the black bear.

Once during the spectacular caribou migrations that took place across the upper Yukon River, I watched a black bear get caught up in a great swimming herd that stretched from bank to bank. So thick were the caribou in the mile-wide current that a paddle-wheel steamer on which I was a passenger had to tie up at the river's edge to let the animals complete their crossing.

It was a thrilling sight and we were all enjoying the wonder of it when, suddenly, someone shouted, "Bear!"

Just a few feet ahead of several hundred bull caribou, carrying their huge antlers aloft like upended rocking chairs while swimming high out of water with extraordinary speed, we saw the black bear sunk to its ears struggling valiantly to stay ahead. It wasn't any use. Spurred on by the shouting passengers, the stampeding caribou surged over the bear and I watched it vanish under a thousand flaying hoofs. My binoculars picked it up again far downstream. It was barely awash in the turbid currents, wallowing weakly as though it were more dead than alive.

On the same river-steamer trip we saw another black bear, this one a mother with three cubs racing from the water's edge up a steepening sandbank to a point where forward progress was no longer possible. With hind feet combing their ears at every jump, the family scrambled madly to reach the overhanging top. It just couldn't be done. As the steamer's paddle wheels thrashed around a bend in the Yukon I took one last look at all four bears spinning their wheels in the soft sand.

Like other bear species, the omnivorous black ones fit their enormous appetites to the food most available at the time and place. In the fall season those along the Yukon gorged themselves on wild rose apples, lingonberries, and sweet blueberries, supplemented by fish from the creeks, ground squirrels, offal, and such other wild game as they can kill. The dark, greasy flesh of the beaver is a choice item and the bears move with incredible stealth from one beaver lodge to another to ambush the busy inmates as they toil at their tree-cutting and dam-building. Indian fur-trapper Johnny Taska told me how one of these beaver-killing bears almost killed him, too.

Johnny was paddling a birchbark canoe quietly along a small slough one spring, rifle resting across the thwarts ready for a quick shot at any beaver that showed above the surface. He had already scored once, and the carcass had been placed in the bow of the canoe to offset his own weight in the stern. As Johnny came to a turn where the brush overlapped across the narrow waterway, a bear leaped off the high bank, landed on the dead beaver and shot right on through the frail shell of birchbark. The canoe sank immediately. Johnny said he caught one brief glimpse of the bear floundering ashore with the beaver in its jaws, before he went under. Later, he managed to salvage his rifle, but never again laid eyes on the bear or the beaver.

Adult black bears tend to be loners except during the honeymoon period, which begins for the female in her third summer, lasts a couple of weeks, and does not occur again for two full years. The actual mating may come about after several days of companionship, or may happen with dramatic suddenness. On a late June day veteran Kenai Peninsula guide Hank Lucas and I reclined against our packboards watching through our field glasses as an unusually large boar stood on its hind feet sniffing the breezes with absorbing interest. Suddenly, it dropped to all fours and started toward us at a furious gallop. Surprised, I reached for my rifle, but Hank said "No!"

He'd seen something I hadn't. There was another scent in its nostrils as it swept by us, and I had to follow its headlong flight to learn the attraction. It was the aroma of a she-bear at the peak of her oestrus period, and the big bear was responding with all speed.

Its haste was entirely unnecessary. The ardent female wasn't going anywhere. Instead, she swung about to greet her onrushing swain, bit him gently on the neck and stood compliantly for his embrace. After a while we saw her leading the way up over a ridge and out of sight, the male following as meekly as a dog on a leash. A week later Hank and I spotted the same pair. One small change had taken place. This time the boar was leading and the she-bear following. Grinned the Kenai guide wryly, "Alla same Indian marriage."

One of the oddest bear-connected situations I ever blundered into was at a lumber camp on an island off the British Columbia coast. The logging crews had all flown into the city of Victoria to celebrate the Queen's birthday, leaving only a crippled old watchman and a savage police dog to guard a score or more of tar-papered shacks from the bold inroads of half-tame black bears. As I walked up the trail to the first of the huts, the police dog came bounding silently toward me with bared teeth. Then, suddenly, its manner changed. Though I was a total stranger, the dog trotted up to me with wagging tail to nose my hand like an old friend.

The old watchman came hobbling out of the cookhouse to explain. "The bears have been driving Prince crazy," he said.

"No sooner does he chase them away from one shack when more bears show up at the other end of the camp. The job is too much for one dog; they're running him ragged. He's so hoarse he can't bark any more, and he hopes you've come to give him a little help."

Breaking and entering is a common complaint lodged against the black bears. The most flagrant case came to my attention in Fairbanks, Alaska, back in the days of prohibition. My informant was the town's favorite bootlegger, at the moment languishing in a jail cell. He said he didn't expect me to believe his story, because he couldn't believe it himself.

But corroborating evidence gathered by Federal agents who moved in to seize the remains, indicated that a bear with willful intent had broken into the stillhouse during the owner's absence and committed the following acts, to wit: eaten a barrel of fermented mash; spilled a keg of molasses and rolled in it; ripped open a goosedown sleeping bag; bashed in a barrel of flour and flung it all over the room; imbibed unknown quantities of hooch; pulled down the stove-pipe; jumped on a red-hot stove.

At this point the moonshiner arrived on the scene. He was just in time to see the hot-footed bear—all floured and feathered like a monster out of a horror movie—come crashing through the window and, carrying the frame around its neck, vanish into the Alaska solitudes.

"Shoot?" shouted the befuddled prisoner. "Mister, bullets wouldn't have stopped the thing I saw!"

q Father of the Bears

The grizzly bear started "seeing the world" from somewhere in Europe. As it padded its way into new environments, it slowly developed into many forms and various color combinations. Several years ago United States authority Dr. C. Hart Merriam named 69 species and subspecies in North America alone, some of them from minor differences in skull formation and teeth, and some from examination of a single specimen. In the world, the number of such "new bears" rose to 232. Professors with magnifying glasses in hand were eagerly scanning dead bears' teeth and splitting bear hairs when the whole thing was brought to a halt.

The current trend among most zoologists is to recognize but one major species of grizzly ranging across Europe, Asia, and North America. That one species is *Ursus arctos*, Latin designation for the European brown bear. The multiple types springing from father *arctos* are mostly regarded as "mutations" brought about by having to scrounge for different kinds of food in varying habitats. For example, a grizzly dwelling in a gloomy rain forest, catching salmon out of the rivers, would in generations evolve into a beast quite unlike that of another grizzly who roamed among the treeless mountain tops, digging out tiny mice and ground squirrels to fill its belly. The first bear would become coarsely furred, its color dark, and its size very large because of abundant food. The second bear's coat would be silkier in texture due to wind and sun, lighter in hue, and its size would be much smaller because of limited food. The red-flesh diet would also tend to give it a nastier disposition. But both these grizzlies and the hundreds of other variants would be the progeny of the same European brown bear.

Members of the bear family are particularly susceptible to these changes. From the creation of earliest forms 25 or 30 million years ago in the Oligocene, the bear-dogs, as they were first called, have been subject to individual differences in the same litters. As a result, the bear quickly adapts to strange conditions. In the Russian forests it has become an immense, very deep brown or black, heavily furred beast. In the open hills of Kamchatka it is cream-colored. In the high woodlands of Batang the Chinese have a gunnysack-colored bear with a white collar and a black stripe along its back. They call it *Ma hsiung*, the horse bear. It digs holes like a gigantic badger as it searches among the meadows and rock-slides for mouse-hares. The Tibetans won't kill it because they consider *Ma hsiung* "first cousin to man." But it is actually only another deviant from the common European brown bear.

Norway used to figure it had three different kinds of brown bears. Maybe it still does. One was the typical European brown bear. Another was very large, mainly vegetarian in food habits, and was not at all aggressive. Another was blackish-furred, killed and ate horses, and was very savage, indeed. But the Norsemen have been hard put to keep their three bears in separate categories because where their ranges overlapped the brutes paid no attention to one another's cranium shapes or back teeth, but hybridized with pleasure and fertility. So, how many bears did the Norwegians really have? Just one, insists the modern zoologist: the European brown bear.

Precisely where this parent of the world's grizzlies was itself created may never be known. Its bones have been found with the giant cave bears in Montsaunes, France, in company with apes, rhinos, elephants, and hyenas. Even then, roughly ten million years ago, it was quite distinct from the enormous, long-muzzled cave bear. From hereabouts, the European brown bear has been traced southward through the Pyrenees where it still exists as the main supply for bicycle-riding performers in the circus. Other trainable bears also come out of Serbia and the U.S.S.R. On its conquest of the Northern Hemisphere at a time in history when man fled from its wrath, the bear moved through the Middle East, even crossing to Africa dry-footed when the Dark Continent was connected with the Eurasian land mass. Up until forty years ago a form of the European brown bear known as the Crowther grizzly is presumed to have existed in the Atlas Mountains of Egypt. In Africa, too, strange tales are told about a big-snouted bearlike beast called the Karrai, which the natives of Abyssinia claim to have hunted to extinction. In Kenya, this tale is matched with the "Nandi-bear" of unbridled ferocity, of which many folk stories exist, but unfortunately no specimens.

On his historic mission to China, Marco Polo described a "white-spotted" bear of pugnacious character. Back in biblical times a smallish, bold beast of 300 pounds with rust-colored hair and white ring around its neck raided the vineyards from the Holy Lands between the Caucasus to Palestine, and figured in the story of Elisha. Though it is called the Syrian bear all through southern Eurasia, its parentage was in the basic European brown bear, *Ursus arctos*.

Admiration and fear marked the attitude of early humans toward the grizzly. Long before California adopted for its state insignia the golden bear—which it ruthlessly destroyed —the Russians had made the bear their national emblem and hailed it as "the beast that walks like a man."

Under the czars the hunting of the Russian bear was a sport for the nobility. It was usually carried on during the winter after peasants had tracked the great beast to its den. Prodded into raging wakefulness, the huge animal came roaring out of its snow-covered lair to face a ring of guns and spears.

But Emperor Joseph of Austria regarded the bears as outlaw characters and in 1788 decreed their extermination. East Prussia shot its last bear in 1804, and by 1850 bears were wiped out in most parts of Europe. Only in hard-to-reach parts of Switzerland, the Abruzzi Mountains in Italy, and possibly among remote peaks in the French Alps and Spanish Pyrenees does the European brown bear now exist in a feral state. Toward Asia, the number increases. A small-sized grizzly continues to be spotted from time to time in the hills of Southern Iran and along the Persian Gulf. China has a scattering of bears around Yaloong, Yangste, Mekang, and along the Yunnan border. Kashmir has a brown bear of its own, and the slopes of the Himalayas are inhabited by at least two somewhat dissimilar types. Many naturalists who refuse to play games, bluntly state that tracks left behind by the "Abominable Snowman" have a way of leading to excavations dug into the burrows of the pika, a favorite bear morsel. They conclude that the tracks are sun-distorted pad prints of a reddish-colored form of the European brown bear.

Some of these descendants of the basic *Ursus arctos* weigh no more than 200 pounds; others more than 1600. The size is determined by scarcity, or abundance, of food. The color is a matter of achieving a protective hue to match the bear's surroundings. The white polar bear lives against a background of eternal ice and snow. The yellow hair of the mountain grizzly blends well with the seared grasses above the tree line. The dark forms are color-keyed to the shadows of the deep forests.

When the European brown bear reached Japan and the eastern shores of Siberia it had doubtless already evolved into a beast of many shades, shapes, and weights. There is in these recent times an almost white grizzly in the Kurile Islands, and there are many smaller, darker bears as well. Along the coast of Okhotsk Sea and its salmon spawning rivers there is said to be a bear of a size and a power to challenge our famous Kodiak brownie, though it is apparently much lighter in color.

Where a 70-mile channel of swirling sea water now separates the continents of Asia and North America at their northern tips, there once existed an isthmus across which many mammals had probably already made their ways to and fro before the bears—who had to spend almost six months of each year in sleep—arrived on the scene. By the time the European brown bear reached the prehistoric land bridge across Bering Strait, it must have been a well-traveled thoroughfare for woolly mammoths, mastodons, regal bisons, camels, horses, giant elk-moose, deer, caribou, antelope, and for pursuing predators like wolves, huge lions, and fierce sabre-toothed cats.

In the dim distance the bears may have seen the towering mountains where they were to attain their greatest numbers and varieties on the planet, or caught its fresh scent in their nostrils. Soon afterward, the first of the bear scouts, fearing no other creature on earth, swaggered eastward into the new world.

The time: about 100,000 years ago.

9 Monarch of the American Wilderness

Though the grizzly bear, *Ursus horribilis*, dominated the New World wilderness for countless centuries it never extended its reign to the Atlantic coast. The course of our early history might have been violently altered if our Gentle Founding Fathers, the Pilgrims, had encountered these huge beasts at Plymouth Rock in 1620 and tried to shoot it out with their blunderbuss fowling pieces. But it was the good fortune of the peaceful colonists that the dreaded "yellow bear" was never found east of Minnesota, Nebraska, Kansas, or Texas. From this line west to the Pacific and north through Canada and Alaska, the fearless grizzly regularly waged war on the Indian aborigines. It raided their tepee villages, scattered the inhabitants, helped itself to their food caches, and when it departed with a full belly it left maimed and slain warriors behind.

In the year of 1795 Sir Alexander MacKenzie, the bold Canadian explorer, wrote: "The Indians entertain great apprehension of this grizzly bear and never venture to attack it except in a party."

A contemporary historian named Brackenridge penned fearfully of the grizzly bear: "This animal is the monarch of the country. The African lion or the Bengal tiger are not more terrible or fierce. He is the enemy of man and literally thirsts for human blood. He seldom fails to attack. The Indians make war upon these ferocious monsters with the same ceremonies as they do with a tribe of their own species, and in the recital of their great victories, the death of a bear gives the warrior greater renown than the scalp of a human enemy. The grizzly possesses an amazing strength and attacks and tears to pieces the largest buffalo . . . ," and so on in a panic of words.

Almost two hundred years elapsed after the Pilgrims landed on the Massachusetts beach before the white man moved far enough west to encounter the swaggering yellow bear. In this period his gunnery equipment improved greatly, though not enough to score clean kills. Oftener than not, the hunters only wounded the savage giants and sent them into frenzies of rage wherein they tried to kill every human they could run down. Long before the dawn of human history, the great beast had roamed unchallenged over the face of western America. It knew no master. Man was its enemy, but not its peer.

The first real clashes of authority between king grizzly and the white strangers from Europe began with the Lewis and Clark expedition that blazed a trail from the Missouri watershed through the Rocky Mountains to the coast of Oregon early in the 19th century. A sample account of a sanguinary meeting is in their diary of May 14, 1805, when the party was still traveling up the Missouri River.

"Toward evening the men in the hindmost canoe discovered a large brown bear lying in the open ground about three hundred paces from the river. Six of them, all good hunters, immediately went to attack him, and concealing themselves by a small eminence, came unperceived within forty paces of him. Four of the hunters now fired and each lodged a ball in his body, two of them directly through the lungs. The furious animal sprang up and ran open-mouthed upon them."

The journal goes on to say, "Two of the hunters who had reserved their fire, then opened up, retarding the beast only momentarily, and they were obliged to flee for their lives. Before they reached the river the bear had almost overtaken them. Two of them jumped in the canoe, the other four separated, and concealing themselves in the willows fired as fast as they could reload. They struck him several times but instead of weakening the monster, each shot seemed only to direct him toward the hunter; till at last he pursued them so closely that they threw aside their guns and pouches and jumped down a perpendicular bank of about twenty feet into the river. The bear sprang after them and was within a few feet of the hindmost when one of the hunters on shore shot him in the head and finally killed him."

Another entry on the grizzly foe appears under date of June 28, 1805: "The yellow bears have become so exceedingly troublesome they constantly infest our camp during the night. We are obliged to sleep with our arms at our sides."

The grizzlies couldn't win, of course, nor was it in their proud nature to run for cover. After untold generations of ruling the western mountains and plains, exacting tribute from every other living creature—including the Indians—the giant yellow bears could not adjust in time to save themselves from the fire-belching muskets of the white man. Not only would they face the deadly hails of bullets; they even launched counter attacks of their own. Their attempts at reprisal against the invasion of their wilderness brought only swifter and deadlier punishment. Like the Indians, the yellow bears made story book heroes out of the men who destroyed them. Names like Kit Carson, Jim Bridger, Jedediah Smith, Younger, and dozens of others were lauded for their exploits as bear slayers as well as for their Indian killings. Among the latest in the past century to win fame as a grizzly hunter was the bespectacled scholar who went west to gain health and came home to become President Teddy Roosevelt.

The few grizzly bears that escaped the scouts with their cap and ball muzzle-loaders met an even deadlier foe in the buffalo hide-hunters with their powerful Sharp's rifles. The incredibly tragic result was that *within seventy-five years of their first contact with the covered-wagon pioneers, the great yellow carnivores of the American West, monarchs of all they surveyed since the Ice Age, were virtually wiped off the map.*

Of the seventeen western states where a "guesstimated" 100,000 yellow bears once trod supreme, only four can now lay claim to harboring living grizzlies; Montana, Wyoming, Idaho, and Colorado. Once in a while one of the other thirteen western states will hopefully announce the sighting of a grizzly, but for all practical purposes the silver-tipped giant bears are gone forever from their old homes in Washington, Oregon, California, Nevada, Utah, Arizona, New Mexico, Texas, Kansas, Nebraska, Minnesota, North and South Dakota. Excluding Alaska, more than ninety-nine percent of the original grizzly populations of the United States have been destroyed, and the fractional one percent are mostly within the boundaries of our National Parks.

California is one of the saddest examples of thoughtless, total destruction of the beast about which it now thinks highly enough to use as the central figure in its state flag. *Ursus magister,* sometimes called the San Diego grizzly, but far better known as the golden bear, was one of the most strikingly beautiful of all American predators. It was, furthermore, one of the largest, if not actually the largest, of all grizzlies ever to roam the earth! In the Santa Ana and San Jacinto Mountains where it was once abundant, any number of golden bear records attest individual weights of 1,400 pounds. Kern County once boasted of a 2,000 pound bear!

At the outbreak of the Civil War the golden bear and its six closely related California subspecies were very plentiful where the city of Stockton now stands. They ranged up the river valleys through Yuba City and on up the Sacramento River past Redding into the Shasta Mountains. Today, hundreds of California communities brag about the big bears they used to have. They point with pride to the golden bear emblem as something special for their state. But a hundred years ago this noblest of all carnivores was treated like the yellow plague and destroyed without mercy.

Every man who killed one was acclaimed a public bene- factor. When John Sutter discovered gold in 1848 and adven- turers from all over the world started pouring into California, the incentive to shoot every grizzly on sight became even greater. The hunters didn't have far to look. Golden grizzlies lined the shores of San Francisco Bay and the nearby river banks. Soon, bear carcasses hung like dressed beef in the local markets, and bear steaks fetched fancy prices from the Forty- niners. To further gratify the whims of newly-rich miners, fights to the death were staged between chained grizzlies and Spanish bulls.

Whereas the original Indian tribes had been content to or- ganize war parties to repel the *Uzumati* (grizzly) from their villages, the white newcomers demanded no less than death penalties. Big print in the newspapers of that day stressed the awesome ferocity of the golden bear:

"Grizzly kills several people at Carmel Mission."

"Three men killed by grizzlies in Monterey Bay."

"So many grizzlies no one dares to go about after dark."

This at Eel River junction with the Van Duzen, 1852: "So many grizzlies schools closed because unsafe for children to use trails."

Shasta County: "Bears in groups of 8 and 10."

Coast Range: "Unpleasantly abundant."

From a high point in Mattole County: "Man counts 40 bears."

Merced River below Yosemite: "Many grizzlies. Man- zanita and scrub oak thickets so dense they can never be driven out."

Marysville Buttes: "Dangerously infested."

Firearms and traps deemed insufficient measures. "In desperation the ranchers have started poisoning every bear carcass to kill more bears."

The tide of this strange battle between settlers and the yellow bears turned swiftly and tragically. In the year of 1875 Mendocino County suddenly announced that it had wiped out its last grizzly.

Ten years later, in 1885, Salinas Valley joined the proud ranks of California communities that had eradicated their grizzlies. The last golden bear died from eating poisoned tallow baits. Humboldt County hung out the "all clear—no more grizzlies" banner in 1890. The rest of the state quickly emulated its three leading counties.

The last photograph believed to have been taken of a live California grizzly was snapped in San Francisco's Golden Gate Park in 1899. The enormous beast, estimated to weigh as much as 1600 pounds, had been trapped by a Mexican ten years earlier. When "Monarch" became decrepit and was shot in its cage in May of 1911, California's claim to the "largest bear ever held in captivity" died with it. Though the end was plainly in sight for the rest of its golden bears, the state made no effort to save them.

In August of 1901 an enormous golden bear weighing almost three-quarters of a ton was shot at the head of Onofre Canyon. It took the exterminators seven more years to track down and kill its mate.

In 1916 a man by the name of Cornelius B. Johnston is said to have discovered, trapped, and then shot the famous Sunland grizzly within half a mile of his home in the lower part of Tujunga Canyon in Los Angeles County.

The final chapter in the living history of the golden bear, the California insignia so proudly flaunted today, was written shortly afterward. The last verified occurrence of a grizzly was at Horse Corral Meadows, Tulare County, in August of

1922. A man by the name of Jesse B. Agnew was accorded due honors for shooting it dead.

When it was all over, when California had been made safe from all people-killing bears, when a tremendously valuable attraction had gone into oblivion with the great auk and the passenger pigeon—a thoughtful Californian made a remark I shall always remember.

"All the humans slain by California's golden bears in 75 years," he said, "probably would not equal the number now killed and maimed on our highways during a holiday weekend."

¶ North and West with the Grizzly

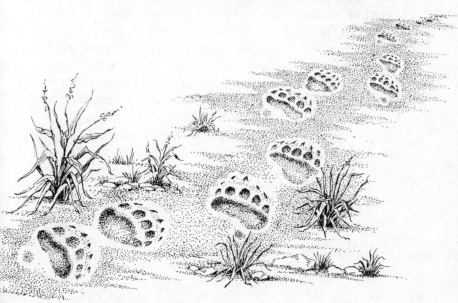

Oregon and Washington were equally determined to wipe out their big bears. In the year of 1806 when the Lewis and Clark expedition blazed the Oregon Trail through to salt water, the giant yellow bears were deemed a constant hazard. The bold carnivores prowled the Siskiyou Mountains, forming the present boundary between California and Oregon, and policed the stream banks as if they owned every salmon in the rivers. Their padded pathways lined the Klamath, Rogue, Umpqua, Willamette, and the great Columbia—the first roads used by the pioneers. Grizzlies raided the summer fish camps of the Indians and sent whole families fleeing for their lives. Only the rashest of incoming whites journeyed alone. If a beaver trapper failed to show up at the trading post, he was likely to be written off the ledger as "killed by a grizzly."

Old woodcuts in Oregon's early nineteenth century periodicals frequently depicted shaggy behemoths the size of hairy mammoths rearing on their haunches and with blood dripping off enormous fangs as they bashed in the skulls of puny creatures like saddle horses, riders, and domestic bulls. Grave doubts were expressed whether the covered-wagon pioneers would ever be able to save their livestock or even their children from such bellowing monsters and those slavering jaws. Considering Oregon's small human population through much of the 1800's, it produced a bumper crop of bear tales featuring heroes and liars who have not been properly sorted out to this day.

The grizzly made a colorful splash in Oregon's history, but now when the ripples have died away, we find that the saga of the yellow bear's grim stand against the encroaching white homesteader can really be told under three datelines spaced half a century apart.

1811: Grizzly bears abundant, wide ranging and extremely ferocious.

1845: Grizzly bears rated as worst public enemy. Trailed and shot by posses of livestock owners. Professional bear killers hired by ranchers. Bear meat on every table; esteemed as food. Leaving river bottoms and retreating into high peaks.

1933: A lone yellow bear sighted slinking along the upper Willamette. Believed to be the last living grizzly ever seen in Oregon.

Though Washington State once boasted a dark, coastal grizzly that made life interesting for the harpoon-carrying Salish Indians camped along the salmon-filled rivers, and a lighter, hump-shouldered type armed with long claws for digging mountain marmots out of their burrows, the doom of both types was sealed when the first white settlers drove their herds of sheep and cattle into the new land. Parties of men armed with the new repeating rifles delivering streams of heavy lead slugs, overpowered every grizzly they could surround. Only the small human population of early Washington—in 1860, for example, it had less than 12,000 residents and was still a part of Oregon Territory—provided the grizzly a few extra years to survive.

In 1833 a man hunting out of Spokane claimed he saw eleven grizzlies during one short hunt. As late as the year of 1923 a desperate old renegade bear with a price on its head went down in a burst of grizzly glory by slaughtering 35 head of cattle and 150 sheep in the wild Okanogan range country. It was the last of the grizzly clan's battle to stave off the white man. Sagging under the weight of bullets delivered by practically every rancher in the hills, the old outlaw finally sank to the ground. It is said to have tipped the scales—belly full of mutton and hide full of lead slugs—at 1,100 pounds!

Neither Oregon nor Washington has permitted sentiment to interfere with the business of raising meat for market. "You can't have both beef cattle and grizzly bears on the same range," they declare and there aren't enough wildlife lovers to argue the point. When someone hopefully suggests restoring a few grizzlies for old times' sake, the ranchers hit the roof. "Good riddance! We don't want any more grizzlies." And then they say it: *There's no room for grizzlies any more.*

Today, the big bear, if it occurs at all in Washington, is a rare wanderer from Canada or from one of the four Rocky Mountain states where they still hang on. With Yellowstone National Park leading the census with 150 protected silver-tipped bears, there is a population of from 500 to 1,000 thinly spread through the wilder portions of Montana, Wyoming, Idaho, and Colorado. Though there is some public shooting allowed, a more popular type of "gunning" grizzlies is that carried on by the famous Craighead brothers, John and Frank, in Yellowstone Park. Using dart guns loaded with a curare-like drug called succinylcholine chloride and doing their shooting generally within fifteen or twenty paces, they manage to put the bears to sleep long enough to tattoo them for permanent identification and decorate their ears with colored markers for binocular observation in the wild. Some are even tagged with radio transmitters giving off a pulsed signal pinpointing their exact location day after day.

When someone asks the brothers why they risk their lives in this kind of derring-do—"What good is a grizzly, anyway?" —the Craigheads respond thoughtfully. "Because when the grizzly is gone, he's gone forever, and we can't make another one."

They might have added that it took nature millions of years to evolve the grizzly from the grotesque dog-bear of the Oligocene, and now in less than a century it's almost gone in the United States. There are only two regions on the continent where the grizzly bear is not presently endangered, and these are among the roadless mountains of western Canada and Alaska.

Beginning just above the northern abutment of Idaho and Montana with the Canadian provinces of British Columbia and Alberta, thence extending upward along the backbone of the upper Rocky Mountains to bisect Yukon and Northwest Territories, is the largest remaining grizzly habitat left in America. It is a vast region, largely uninhabited except in the south end, roughly 1,600 miles long by 400 miles wide. It takes in the Banff and Jasper snow peaks and embraces huge Tweedsmuir Park in the Coast mountains. The wild headwaters of the Peace and Liard Rivers, draining into the Arctic Ocean and one of the richest big-game fields in the world, are close to the center of this grizzly haven. A separated string of frigid summits known as the Mackenzie Mountains, part of which are within the Arctic Circle, is inhabited by what must be the hardiest grizzlies on earth. Most of the tall country through which they wander is free of ice and snow for no more than three or four months of the year. The mercury drops to 70 degrees below zero in the winter, and the grizzly must spend two-thirds of its life curled in its den under tons of drifted snow.

But the very harshness of this boreal mountain range has in it the special qualities to insure long life to its grizzlies. The climate is too severe for stock ranching, now or ever. Human communities are small and widely scattered, and gun-toting men seldom penetrate this remaining kingdom of the mountain silver-tip. For a few years—perhaps for many—the grizzly should find in this lofty cold land room to live their kind of life.

That life for the most part is to wander alone, feeling little urge to be with its own kind except at mating time, fearing no other wild creature. One of the mountain grizzly's favorite spots is a steep sidehill inhabited by colonies of hoary marmots. Pressing its nose against the slide rock to pinpoint the prey, the mountain grizzly huffs and puffs as it flings rocks aside to expose the fat whistler. Spotted ground squirrel push-up mounds with connecting runways will engage the silver-tip for hours on end, excavating like a steam shovel, grabbing and bolting furry morsels, then excavating some more until the whole area looks as if it had been churned by a bulldozer. The mountain breezes will freight the decaying odors of winter-killed caribou and mountain sheep to its nostrils for long distances. With this carrion, the grizzly will mix a fair amount of fresh game captured—sometimes—after a belly-crawling stalk and furious closing rush. Most big-game animals, if they are healthy and active, will elude this final charge; but to the sick, the very old or the very young, it is the end.

A prodigious quantity of wild berries go down the gullet of a Canadian mountain silver-tip during the summer season. A homesteader's wife said she watched a big grizzly work over a carpet of tart red lingonberries above their cabin on the upper Yukon. After the bear had moved uphill, the lady went out to gather her own supply before the beast got them all. Covering approximately the same size area as the grizzly, her filled buckets contained 17 quarts! Nor had the grizzly yet satisfied its gargantuan appetite; it had simply switched to sweeter fare. It had waddled up the slope to a patch of honey-sweet blueberries, and the lady said she could see it working its big nose back and forth like a vacuum cleaner until darkness hid it from view.

A hairy old-timer living almost like a bear himself in the deep Canadian bush told me a hungry man could learn a lot about keeping his belly full by watching the grizzly. Almost everything it eats, he insisted, could be stomached by a man— bulbs, roots, green shoots, mushrooms, grasses, shrubs, bark, and a long list of mammals from moose to mice, supplemented by birds' eggs, fledglings, fishes, ants, and beetles. "The silvertip is a real rustler," said the hermit of the bush country admiringly. "He knows how to keep his ribs padded with fat."

The loner showed me a skinned carcass hanging in his cache and invited me to share a platter of sourdough hot cakes fried in bear lard stripped off its intestines. They were tasty and oily, and so were the remarkably tender grizzly steaks he dished up that evening, though I would not go so far as to call them habit forming.

There is a wide variation between the brown salmon-eaters of British Columbia's coastal streams and the high-shouldered silver-tips of the interior mountains stretching far into the Arctic Zone. The Canadians have chosen to blanket them all under the name of grizzly. They realize that subspecies certainly exist, but say they cannot be designated until the group is given systematic revision. They remember well the case of the "Patriarchal Bear" named in 1918 by our C. Hart Merriam on the basis of a single, unique lower second molar found in the central barren lands of the Mackenzie District. Dr. Merriam's publications of a new bear species under the Latin name of *Vetularctos inopinatus* was for many years hailed as a valuable scientific contribution about an exceedingly rare creature. Recently, following scrutiny of many more specimens from that isolated part of the Arctic, the National Museum of Canada has been forced to cross *Vetularctos* off its catalog.

"The so-called 'Patriarchal Bear' is," writes Director A. W. F. Banfield, "a strikingly beautiful beast with its long, woolly, buffy coat and sharply contrasting rufous underparts and legs. But it is merely a color phase of the grizzly." And so ends a legend.

Somewhat similar grizzlies, shading from pure creamy white through yellow to tan, with cleanly separated trim colors ranging from reddish-brown and chocolate to ebony black, have been sighted in the Richardson Mountains west of Canada's Peel River. These tundra, or barren-land grizzlies as they are sometimes called, also inhabit a range known as the British Mountains, which merge into the Alaskan Brooks Range and extend west for 700 miles to Cape Lisburne before dipping steeply into the Arctic Ocean to reappear as the Anadyr Range in Siberia. In this enormous stretch of jumbled, ice-capped peaks the grizzly should find room to live long after the sheltering timber of its Southeastern Alaska homes have been fed to the pulp mills.

¶ Kootznahoo, Home of the Bears

I'd spent enough time among the bears with the famous Alaska guide Hosea Sarber to realize this would be a day of danger. It was during the second week of our bear census in the dark wilderness of Admiralty Island, known to the Indians as *Kootznahoo,* Home of the Bears. We left our anchored patrol vessel at daybreak, rowed our skiff to the river mouth and began wading upstream toward an experience I have never forgotten.

Sarber, with his .30-06 rifle cradled across his arm in case of sudden attack, led the way. I followed with a bucket of plaster of Paris for casting sample bear tracks. Salmon so filled the shallows there wasn't room to set our boots without touching off a flurry of splashes. On the gravel shores, eagles and ravens and gulls haggled over the salmon scraps left by the bears.

It would be like this, Sarber said, all the way upriver for three miles to a point where we could see a cataract leaping off a flat mountain-top, bouncing from ledge to ledge and finally disappearing among the tree tops. At the bottom of this waterfall we'd find an almost solid mass of humpback and dog salmon churning and hurling themselves at the thudding column of snow water. In this mist-filled evergreen jungle, where scarcely a human had ever made a footprint, there'd be a concentration of salmon—and of sour-tempered grizzly and brown bears unequaled for variety and numbers anywhere else in the world.

That was why Sarber planned to reach the falls at sun high, when most of the bears would have had their morning fill of fish and be bedded down in the timber. We'd already worked out a formula for counting the bears without seeing them. We'd discovered that their pad prints were as individual as human fingerprints. Some were hamshaped, some oval, and some almost as narrow as the track of a human. Each track showed scratches, pore patterns, twisted and broken claws unlike those of any other bear. We recognized the cubs because their pad marks measured only four inches wide, whereas the old, half-ton boars left deep impressions we couldn't cover with our hats.

We wouldn't kill a bear unless we had to. In fact, it would be all right with us if we didn't even see one all day. But ten minutes later a rust-colored hulk erupted from the river with a salmon in its jaws, ambled ashore, and faced us across a gravel bar no more than forty paces away. Never taking its eyes off us for a moment, the bear spread itself flat across the stones like a wet rug and devoured its fish, leaving head, tail and backbone for the two gulls that were hopping and screaming within inches of its chomping jaws. Only after it had finished its meal did the bear turn its back on us and stroll casually into the forest shadows.

Hosea, who disagreed with the naturalists who credited five species of grizzly and brown bear to Admiralty Island, nevertheless made a stab at nomenclature. "Near as I can tell," he said, "that was the bear that Dr. C. Hart Merriam classed as *Ursus mirabilis,* the strange grizzly. It's trigger-tempered and unpredictable like all the grizzlies, but it isn't as big and dangerous as another one we'll be running into up at the falls."

He waited while I mixed a batch of plaster and poured it into a hind track. "Old native name for the big brute is Black Hoots, the Killer," he offered. "The Indians weren't just flapping their lips, either, because I've helped carry some of its victims out of the woods on stretchers."

I lifted the plaster cast, an operation Hosea regarded with tolerant amusement, and marked it for identification. We moved on upstream past well-trodden bear trails leading down off the timbered spurs to the river. On either side of us the banks were cluttered with grizzly tracks, and their tunnelings led through salmonberry patches from one river bend to the next.

Beyond the last muskeg, Sarber watched carefully as he slipped along in the permanent gloom of the great spruce trees, the moss-draped hemlocks and old growth cedars. Their branches laced together across the river, leaving only occasional open patches through which the sun shafts came probing like searchlights to illuminate the hordes of spawning salmon. Schools of red-spotted Dolly Varden trout snapped at the pea-sized eggs floating among the thrashing humpies and dogs. The shadows were alive with flapping wings and shrieking birds come to join the summer feast. There were mysterious rustlings of unseen things in the understory of brier and devil's-club thickets. It was an eerie place where a bear attack could come in a split second.

Though we had seen but one bear, we'd passed the sign of at least twenty others that had winded us and chosen to steal quietly into the cover of the forest. Twice we saw sprinkled trails leading from the river across the dry pebbles, and once as we cut over a sandbar Sarber laid a forefinger against his lips and pointed to salmon in our path. A bite had been taken out of its back and it was still kicking.

As we neared the base of the cataract the stream canyon became almost opaque with mist. Giant trees wore swaying shrouds of gray moss. It was a place for bears, I thought, not people, and then a sudden squalling of gulls and ravens ahead brought Hosea's thumb to the safety of his rifle. But by the time we came sloshing around the river's turn there was nothing in sight except a hassle of birds around another flopping fish. My eyes were scanning about for a clean-cut pad print in the silt when Hosea spoke out of the corner of his mouth. "You want to see the biggest dang brute on the island, turn around real slow and look behind you."

I swung my head, not slow but fast, because I'd already caught a flash of its movement. It had pushed soundlessly out of the devil's club, and now it reared up alongside a big waterlogged snag to study us, then dropped back on all fours. When my eyes met it full I couldn't help gasping. The animal was huge; it was black as a load of coal, and for all its bulk appeared to be nimble as a cat. It was a fearsome sight, yet Sarber did not shoot. He had noticed that the rounded ears of the beast were fanned erect, not buttoned back like those of a bear in a killing rage. Its teeth clacked loudly and drops of foam fell from its jaws, but the sideways hops it made toward us were more bluster than the headlong charge of a bear in full attack, and it appeared to be kicking up an unnecessary fuss in the water as it bounced nearer.

When it reached a shallow spot fifty feet away it jumped up and down stiff-legged until it had swatted the pool into bubbles, then abruptly froze in its tracks and glared at us like a giant ogre. Sarber, with rifle sights lined up on a spot between the two burning eyes, spoke comforting words. "The black devil is bluffing." But his cheek remained pressed against his rifle stock. "Maybe," he added. The great bear could

change moods in an instant and we both knew it. If the ears
of the bear went down, if it started licking its tongue across
its lips, if it lowered its enormous head, if it came any closer,
Sarber would have to shoot.

An accident broke the spell. The tin bucket suddenly
slipped from my sweaty fingers and rolled clattering across
the sloping rocks toward the river. The bear gave a startled
huff! Neither of us moved a muscle as the monster swung its
head ponderously, took another long look at us, then shuffled
slowly away. Its shaggy rump looked as big and unreal as a
hairy mammoth's as it disappeared into the underbrush. Sarber was only partly satisfied. "We'll see that big boy again,"
he promised.

Below the falls another sight as undisturbed by civilization
as if it were still in the Ice Age greeted us. The pounding water
of the lofty cataract had ground a deep basin out of solid
granite, and it was now choked with salmon that had unknow-
ingly reached the end of the line for them. Already past the
last spawning gravel in the river, they continued to jump
blindly, battering their shining bodies against the wet rocks,
only to be hurled back into the boiling caldron where tons of
them went washing around and around in a slithering mass.

Two yearling grizzlies, soaked as drowned rats, were dodging in and out of the showering falls, catching and releasing
salmon and galloping over the slippery rocks in a furious game
of tag. They went scooting into the dark timber when they
caught our scent, and later we found enough morning sign to
indicate that at least thirty bears had been feasting on the
doomed fish.

Later, in going over our notes, Hosea and I figured our bear
count for the three-mile stretch of river to be not less than
sixty. If the rest of Admiralty Island's salmon streams aver-
aged as well, we'd wind up our census with close to a thousand
bears for this one island. To make the figures even more astonishing, all the bears were in a National Forest visible to

tourists on steamers plying between Petersburg and Juneau on Alaska's Inside Passage.

"And five kinds of them," I reminded Hosea, though I knew that neither he nor any other Alaska guide would agree with the "experts" who named new subspecies sometimes from examination of a single skull. I started to name the Admiralty bears as listed by Dr. C. Hart Merriam: Island grizzly, Admiralty grizzly, crested bear, strange grizzly . . . Hosea cut me off. For him there was but one bear on Admiralty. It was the massive, almost pure black Shiras bear, one of the most striking-looking predators in existence.

As long as he lived, Hosea Sarber never changed his mind about this dark, brooding giant found only on Admiralty Island. And Ralph Young of Petersburg, the man who succeeded Hosea as the most active bear man in Southeastern Alaska, shares his old friend's views. Like Hosea, Ralph Young scoffs at the "swivel-chair biologists" who ascribe five species of brown and grizzly bears to an island only eighty-five miles long and barely twenty miles wide. Young recognizes, at most, a medium-sized, brownish grizzly weighing from 500 to 700 pounds and the black form weighing half a ton or more at full growth.

"If there are five kinds of bears on Admiralty Island," says Ralph Young wryly, "someone has forgotten to tell the bears about it. I've seen big black ones traveling with little brown ones. I've seen a yellow sow-bear with three cubs of different shadings. I've even seen a blue-colored bear on the island." Adds Young with logic, "I think we ought to give up trying to catalogue the Admiralty bears, because when mating time comes they won't obey the rules. We ought to just go along with the fact that here at the mercy of the United States Forest Service is the greatest collection of grizzly bears the world will ever know. We ought to be more concerned on how this Federal organization protects these bears from its logging crews."

At the base of the thundering falls I could find no pad marks to match those of the giant Shiras black; so while Hosea amused himself by counting salmon-gorged eagles sleeping in the snags I dropped down around the bend with my bucket of plaster. A few feet from a stump I found and measured a hind track 10 inches wide by 14 inches long, not counting the claw marks. I sprayed it with gum arabic, poured in the wet plaster reinforced with strips of cloth, and was waiting for the stuff to set when I became aware of a penetrating stench. For a moment the full meaning of it escaped me. Then, suddenly, I knew fear. The owner of the huge track had stalked me in dead silence. Somewhere, very close, it was watching me.

Fighting a natural urge to get away from there fast, or to yell out to Hosea, either of which could get me killed quickly, I picked up my bucket as casually as I could and began backing slowly toward the river. As I straightened up I found myself staring directly at a broad, black head that looked as big as a wheelbarrow. The bear had been close enough to breathe down my neck as I worked absorbed over its track, and now I was almost within reach of its great hooked claws. But it was the beast's eyes that held me. They were glaring into mine with a malevolence that I had never seen in those of another wild thing.

I must have gasped aloud at the horror of it. The bear's response was to drop heavily from its squatting position to all fours. I had no possible defense in mind other than flinging the bucket of plaster in its face and diving for the river when I heard Sarber's level voice. "Just keep backing away. Easy."

Hosea had come around the bend, pebbles crunching steadily under his boot soles. The black brute watched his every step until we converged at the water's edge. At that instant it covered half the distance between us in two prodigious bounds. It skidded to a stop in a crashing of stones and let go with belly-deep coughs that echoed through the forest. As it faced us stiff-legged, jaws clacking, I was confident that Hosea could have split its skull with a single bullet, because he was a cool, deadly shot. But he had the ice-water judgment to hold his fire.

It wasn't until we had managed a further retreat to the middle of the river that Hosea spoke again. He said he guessed we were in the clear if we kept moving along and didn't stop for any more foolishness with the plaster bucket. It was midafternoon, I remember. All the bears on the river were heading down from their beds in the timber to fish through the twilight hours.

We sloshed downcurrent, keeping well out from the brush-screened banks. After a while Hosea said somewhat illogically, "You know, these bears really are a peaceable lot; they don't want any trouble." He swung around for a look at the giant Shiras bear huffing and snorting its anger on the gravel bar. "Of course, you got to keep out of their way."

I agreed with this latter remark, and then I said something about our having accomplished our mission on the river, anyway; that we'd got everything we went up there for.

"Not quite," said Hosea with sly humor. "You forgot to pick up your plaster bear track."

q The Grizzly Looks at You

Recalling the incident now, I am convinced that the black grizzly of Admiralty Island had no intention of attacking me; otherwise it would have killed me with a single blow of its paw when it stalked me undetected. Hosea said that the big brute realized I was doing something with its track and wanted to find out what I had in mind. Its display of anger and resentment came only after it knew I had discovered its presence.

"The thing about grizzlies is their high intelligence," declared Hosea. "Every one I have ever met in the woods has tried to read my mind. There isn't any question that the grizzly in modern times—since man carries a high-power rifle —recognizes man as a superior sort of beast, though in no way reconciled that he is master. It knows man is dangerous. It wants to know what you're thinking."

Is the man creature going to challenge? Is the two-legged trespasser in its domain merely passing through, or will the bear have to fight for its life? These things a grizzly must decide for itself, must try to reason through its eyes and ears and nose as it peers and listens and sniffs. Sometimes its decisions result in violence and death. Sometimes the wild reasoning of the bear proves to be right.

Like the time a hunter lay in wait at the mouth of a salmon spawning stream on Admiralty Island in Southeastern Alaska. There had been reports that a trophy-sized grizzly came out of the alders every early morning and late evening to catch its fill of migrating fish. This morning the bear didn't show up, so the hunter decided to wait around. He rowed himself out to a sandbar to spend the middle of the day.

In the warmth of high noon he fell asleep. He awakened to hear a soft crunch in the sand and when he opened his eyes he found himself gazing with more than average interest at a hairy leg the size of a tree trunk. Next, a big wet nose was shoved against his cheek, followed by a blast of breath freighted with the odor of fish. Eyes blinked shut, cringing in dread of a blow the like of which could tear the head of an ox loose from its neck, the hunter waited while the bear walked slowly around his prone body. After making a leisurely inspection the bear turned away, paddled across to the river mouth and began chasing salmon in the riffles. By this time the hunter had recovered enough courage to sit up and reach for his rifle. But give him credit for not shooting. He watched until the grizzly vanished into the forest with a salmon dangling from its jaws, then betook himself to his skiff and rowed away. And that night he was very kind to his family.

Four teen-age boys day-napping in a tent in the Alaska Range bear country had a similar experience. One of the lads opened his blue eyes to find a grizzly's head inside the canvas. Soundlessly, the silver-tipped beast looked at each recumbent form and for one spine-shivering moment fastened its hot stare on the horror-bulged eyes of the awakened boy. Then it silently withdrew. The other lads jeered at the "nightmare" until they opened the tent flap. There on the soft earth was a deep imprint almost as big as a turkey platter.

But the grizzly who found its trail to the river blocked by

a tent belonging to old-timer Hank Lucas on the Kenai Peninsula was not merely satisfied to look. In the dead silence of midnight the grizzly shuffled to the one-man tent, filled its nostrils with the offensive man-scent, and cut loose with one blood-curdling roar after another. At the end of a sleepless night Hank parted the canvas flap to find the earth around his tent ringed with the tracks of an enormous bear. Not the one to be bluffed out of his chosen summer home, Hank tried sleeping there again the next night. He shook his head as he told me about it.

"It wasn't any use," he admitted. "The big devil came back every night and called me dirty names. I didn't want to shoot it, because it didn't want to kill me, either. It just wanted me the hell out of there. So I moved."

One summer evening when author Corey Ford and I were fly casting for Dolly Varden trout in a river on Admiralty Island, Ralph Young suddenly whispered to us: "Look behind you. You got company."

At the edge of the wild rye grass no more than a stone's toss away, two young brown bears were watching us with ears cocked quizzically, their heads turning from side to side as we cast, like a pair of spectators at a tennis match. Ralph, squatting on the gravel bar with his .375 rifle resting on his lap, made no move as the yearling rose on their haunches for a better view. "Just curious," he shrugged. "Never saw anybody catching fish without using his teeth. Probably you're the first human beings they ever ran into." He added thoughtfully, "But you won't be the last."

On another occasion when Hosea left me alone while I was casting plaster tracks of the grizzlies, I heard a bear snort angrily in a nearby alder thicket and since I was unarmed I thought it the better part of valor to ascend a tree and watch proceedings from the safety of a limb twenty feet above the ground. After a few moments the grizzly came pushing out into view and swaggered slowly to the plaster-filled track. It studied the white shape with interest, sniffed at my tin bucket, and blasted through its nose distastefully.

Before it turned away, the bear swung its big head upward to let me know it had been aware of me all the time, skinned its lips ever so slightly and trudged away as though completely unconcerned about the whole show. But it wasn't fooling anybody, especially me. From my vantage point I was still able to keep it in view as it swung around behind the first bush and lay down facing the butt of the tree where I was perched. There was no animosity in its manner, just curiosity; and when the sound of Hosea's boots came crunching down the gravel bed a few moments later the bear departed quietly.

This odd mannerism of pretending it doesn't see you is a well-established trait among the grizzly bears, though no two of them will ever react alike to the same situation. I have had a bear look right through me as if I wasn't there, keep swinging its head until it was facing the other way and maintain the pose for fifteen minutes, no doubt alert to any movement I might make. I've had them take advantage of a tree trunk to hide all but one eye, and peek at me through the underbrush. In open country the grizzly, to escape detection, will flatten against the tundra like a rug, from which position it can launch itself with unbelievable speed. The point of all this is that no grizzly is likely to act the same as the one you saw yesterday. They are all individualistic to the extreme, all full of surprises, but all highly inquisitive.

One afternon I was crouched, camera in hand, behind some fallen logs overlooking a dry creek bed much used by traveling bears. A huge grizzly soon appeared. As he ambled by in front of my blind he apparently caught my scent, for his gait stiffened and I saw the hairs on his neck rise slightly, then fall again. He gave no other sign, not even turning his head or quickening his pace as he moved around a bend out of sight. But half an hour later as I rose and turned to leave the blind I found myself looking square into his eyes. He had circled, padded noiselessly into position behind my back, and was watching me in dead silence. I saw no sign of anger; he had decided I was harmless. He had outwitted me and turned the tables, and now his upraised ears and cocked head were asking the question: "Well, how do *you* like being spied on?"

Bear man Allen Hasselborg, who built a small cabin in the heart of Admiralty Island and lived a hermit-like existence among its grizzlies for many years, once related an instance when a visiting photographer came out second best in a stalking contest with a big, gray-tipped she-grizzly. Camera in hand, the photographer waded upstream in the wake of the grizzly and her little cub, hoping to snap a closeup picture. The mother gave not the slightest sign that she was being followed, so it came as a complete surprise to the cameraman when he rounded a bend and saw only an empty stretch of river ahead.

"The fellow started ahead, but I stopped him," said Hasselborg. "From my position in the rear I could see something he couldn't. Besides," added the whiskered homesteader, "I thought I knew what that old lady was up to."

Hasselborg had seen the wise mother hustle her cub off the shallow river into the dark of the timber and send it scooting up a tree where it would remain out of sight until she called it down again. Then she had crept silently back to square accounts with the man she thought was trying to steal her baby.

"He was a very foolish young man," continued Hasselborg, "but a lucky one. The bear was no more than fifteen yards from him, on her haunches behind a blowdown stump. Her teeth were showing, and she was licking her tongue and working her jaws. The photographer didn't see her, and it's a good thing he didn't, because the instant their eyes met I think she would have ripped him to pieces with her meathook claws and fangs."

To illustrate the difference in action between a sow-bear

protecting her cubs and a lone male with no responsibilities except his own, Hasselborg said that on the same day a big grizzly came out in the trail ahead of them, glanced back without apparent recognition, and moved on until it came to a small hemlock. There it stopped to rub its back against a limb, then reared to its full height to tear a great patch of bark loose. It swung boldly around to stare at the two men before dropping and swaggering out of sight among the big trees.

"He'd left his brand high enough so I could barely reach it with the extended muzzle of my rifle," said Hasselborg. "The big fellow didn't want to fight; he just wanted to warn us what we'd be up against if *we* started one."

Some distance below where Hasselborg River drains out of Hasselborg Lake—both named for Admiralty Island's famous old bachelor homesteader—a trout fishing friend of mine said he once walked along the rim of a rocky gorge and suddenly discovered a dark-brown bear paralleling his footsteps on the other side. Though the distance was only about seventy-five feet, the walls of the canyon were so steep it was almost like looking at a captive grizzly in a moated zoo. The fisherman said he was rather enjoying the prickly sensation until he looked ahead and saw a break in the palisades and a well-rutted game trail leading down to a ford across the river.

"I don't know how the situation might have ended," said the angler. "Maybe the bear was only trying to beat me down to a fishing hole. Maybe it had other ideas. I didn't wait to find out. I turned around and hustled back to my skiff and rowed away from there fast."

For all its huge bulk, the grizzly can move through the forest with a shadowy stealth possessed by no human. Almost always, it sees you first. The exception, of course, is in wide-open country where the use of binoculars gives man the advantage. But in the forest it can move without snapping a twig, or if it suits its purpose the bear will suddenly go crashing through the underbrush like a stampeding elephant. Its moods are just as changeable. When well fed, as on a salmon stream, it will cavort like a spring lamb, and it definitely has a sense of humor, I have seen one mince up to a stump, sniff at it delicately, then like lightning deal it a fearful clout with its paw.

When it wants to run a bluff the grizzly will sometimes rise on ramrod-stiff legs, fluff out like an enraged tomcat, and back on all fours, come hopping sideways while glaring at its victim. Nobody guarantees what will happen, but if you can stand your ground quietly, if you can hide the quaver in your voice while you talk to the bear in moderate tones, if you can put on a convincing show of calmness and firmness, the bear's temper *might* suddenly soften. Having given you the business of buttoned-down ears, popping teeth, foaming jaws, belly-deep whuffs and moans, a change *may* come over the shaggy ogre. The ears may snap forward alertly, the big head may cock sideways like a friendly dog's; the bear may, repeat *may*, stroll away feigning complete indifference. Sometimes I think the grizzly can smell the adrenalin glands of a frightened human, and that it likes to play games with them.

Such a beast accosted me while I was whipping a trout stream. I saw it first upriver before it slipped into the brush. A moment later its barrel-sized head came shoving through some overhanging salmonberry bushes not twenty feet away. The head disappeared, and then the bear was downstream sloshing crosscurrent into cover on the other side. After that, complete silence! Having boxed me in, it was apparently content to leave me guessing. When I finally plucked up enough nerve to get out of there, I had no idea where the bear might be lurking.

The man who shoots with a camera is in for at least as many, and often more thrills than the hunter with a rifle, and the most famous of Alaska guides, Andy Simons, has a story to prove the point:

"I had a topnotch professional photographer with me far

out near the base of Pavlof Volcano," he told me, "picking up some footage of the giant Peninsula brown bear. We built a loose blind of shrubs and tall grass on the edge of a salmon stream and had no sooner crawled behind it than the bears started showing up right in front of the lens, some of them not more than forty or fifty feet away.

"They were huge brutes weighing well over half a ton. Plenty dangerous, too, in such close quarters. But my man calmly chewed tobacco and kept right on grinding out the film while I held my rifle ready in case of a charge.

"Of course, the bears soon found out we were in the blind, but paid no attention for a while. Then, suddenly, one of the biggest of the lot made a sudden rush toward our flimsy hide-out, reared up on its hind legs and let go with an explosive *whuf*! like someone had tipped the safety valve on a locomotive. Instantly, the camera stopped. I kept the rifle centered on the bear but didn't shoot because the big brownie seemed more curious than mad. I took a quick look at he cameraman to see what was wrong. He was holding one hand over his mouth and his face was pale green.

" 'What's the matter?' I whispered. 'Scared?'

" 'No,' he whispered right back, 'but I just swallowed my cud of tobacco.' "

q The Dangerous Mother

During a season I spent on Alaska's Kenai Peninsula with resident guide Hank Lucas, I could not help but notice his concern at the sight of mother and cub grizzlies. One day I found out why he avoided close contact with these bear families, and discouraged my attempts at closeup photography. We had located a salt lick much visited by moose during the summer, and Hank helped me set up a small green tent overlooking the site. When the sharp lines of the tent had been softened with cut brush, I mounted the motion picture camera on its tripod inside and dismissed the guide. "Be seeing you back at camp," I said.

But Hank made no move to leave. "You know," he remarked drily, "you are sitting exactly where I was a year ago when a grizzly mother tried to get me." He made himself comfortable where he had a rear view from the blind. "Could happen again."

144

And then, while we waited for the moose to wade out into the salt lick, Hank told me what had happened on that other August day. He was hunched back against his packsack looking through his binoculars when he heard a sniff at his back. A squall of alarm from a cub grizzly was followed by a bellow of surprise from the mother. His own actions were fast, instinctive, and they saved his life. All in one smooth motion, Hank slipped out of his pack straps, picked up his rifle, and jumped over the edge of the cliff to a narrow, jutting ledge. His free arm wrapped itself around a stunted spruce to hold him from falling a hundred feet to the bottom.

There was a scuffling sound from above and his packsack went hurtling past. Then, ten feet above him, the snarling face of the grizzly thrust itself over the edge of the cliff while the animal stared down at him for a moment. The shaggy head drew back, but this bear wasn't content with merely protecting her cubs. She wanted to finish the fight. The next time Hank saw her, she had dropped down to his level a few yards away and was squeezing herself toward him along the narrow shelf, teeth clicking with rage, foam flying from her jaws as it always does when a bear really means business.

Still in his cramped position, Hank somehow managed to draw back the bolt of his rifle, shove a cartridge into the firing chamber, and holding the gun with his free right hand, extended the muzzle. The brown, furry chest was almost within touching distance when he pressed the trigger. Hank offered no further details, but it was enough that he was still here and the bear wasn't.

In a lighter vein was the experience related to me by a gold rush character known as Two-Step Louie, who got his name in the Klondike Stampede of '97 when he offered a painted lady her weight in gold if she could dance him down. Long retired from such frivolity, he was shacked up on Baranof Island seriously growing the biggest set of whiskers in Alaska when brown bear cub trouble fell upon him.

"I am walking along minding my own business," says seventy-year-old Louie, "when I step right onto a she-bear nursing three cubs. At her first roar I just naturally start reaching for altitude and the next thing I know I seem to have floated up to a spruce limb fifteen feet in the air. In another tree a dozen feet away are the cubs, squealing like prodded pigs."

Explains Two-Step Louie, "Now, while baby grizzlies can scamper up a tree trunk like so many squirrels, the old brownie's toenails are so long and blunt she can't climb. So she stays on the ground whetting her teeth on the butt of the tree for a while, then rushes over to coax the cubs down. But the cubs won't budge, and neither will I.

"No telling how long this might go on if I don't get smart. When the old girl rears up again to make a pass at me, I takes off my jacket and drops it in her face. The way she rips it to pieces makes me shudder, but it also gives me an idea. Off comes my checkered shirt which I wads into a ball. 'Okay, you old hellion,' says I, 'clamp your fangs on this.' I touch a match to the shirt and when it is burning good I let it fall into her open jaws."

Says Two-Step Louie, "Cubs, or no cubs, that bear takes off like a Roman Candle."

Most of the attacks on humans by grizzly mothers who are defending their young are by no means humorous. They are grim, bloody affairs in which the she-bear seldom kills, but maims her victims so badly that they must spend days in the hospital and carry scars of the encounter for the rest of their lives. These onsets usually take place when the man, without realizing how it happened, walks between the cubs and the mother. A goodly percentage of the females will fight to the death to keep human hands off their cubs, and oftener than not gives up her own life in the attempt.

In zoos all across the United States there are grizzly bears acquired by first killing the mother. A common procedure, in fact, was to first shoot the nursing she-bear and when the babies came whimpering back to nuzzle her dead body, fling a heavy net over them.

Does anyone question the right of a grizzly female to fight back in the only way that she knows when she thinks man has designs on her nurslings? The odor of humans is the most hated smell she will ever know. If she succeeds in reaching the man and rendering him helpless, she will not tarry, but quickly gather her family together and flee the scene. To her, man is not food, but repellant vermin.

It was with such knowledge in mind that I once received the fright of my life on Baranof Island. Leading the way through a dense growth of prickly devil's-club, followed by two visiting anglers from New York and carrying the only rifle in the party, I was suddenly aware of a low, dark-brown blotch no more than ten feet ahead. The object scuttled through the brush, and in trying to follow its blurred moves with aimed rifle, I found myself completely trapped in a tangle of clinging, interlocking stems. I was struggling desperately in an attempt to thrust the spiny vines aside and tear my shirt sleeves free of the stinging needles, momentarily expecting a roaring explosion of fury from a nearby mother grizzly, when the fishermen behind me shouted an alarm.

The dark-brown creature was coming toward us. I watched helplessly as it came hopping directly at me and squatted almost on the toes of my boots. It was a young bald eagle that had fallen from its nest in a high spruce.

As to the dispositions of the grizzly cubs themselves, Andy Simons once hand-reared a couple of them at his log cabin home on the shores of Kenai Lake. "They were what they ate," declared Andy. "When I fed them on bread and milk and wild berries they would snuggle down together and go to sleep like a couple of angels. When I gave them raw meat they would squall bloody murder and fight each other like little devils."

One of the rarest sights I ever saw in the Alaska wilderness took place above timberline on Admiralty Island one summer day. I was sitting on a rocky ledge possibly a hundred feet above a well-traveled bear trail when twin grizzly cubs suddenly bounded into view. Behind them swaggered the mother, and because my odor rose upward from my vantage point, she was completely unaware of human presence and at peace with the world. When she came to a grassy hummock almost directly beneath me she sprawled in a recumbent position and gave a low call. At once the cubs came loping back, snuffled their black noses into the hair of her breast, found themselves a nipple each, and began sucking lustily.

Fondly, the mother washed each baby head to foot with her tongue, then leaned back and seemed to fall asleep with the sweet ecstasy of the contact. There was a gentleness in her attachment for these burly little roughnecks I had never expected to find in a grizzly bear. To cap it all, she swung her head to one side and sniffed delicately at a single blue-petaled flower.

After the cubs had nursed their fill, the grizzly family moved, exchanging subdued, murmuring sounds that I am sure must have conveyed their feelings of safety and well-being. If they had swung uphill they would surely have picked up my scent, but fortunately they all meandered onto a sloping hillside some distance away and settled down among the lush, sugar-ripe blueberries.

But sometimes during the summer comes a time when the she-bear must mix some discipline with her mother love. I observed an instance of this in a female with three young in the act of crossing a glacial torrent in Alaska's Valley of Ten Thousand Smokes. While the cubs fretted anxiously, the mother picked each one up by the scruff of its neck and ferried it to the other shore. But when they balked at a mere rill a few moments later, the grizzly parent spanked her whining brats soundly on their rumps and sent them bawling through the shallows. She knew where to draw the line on pampering.

Another time, Hosea Sarber and I watched through our fieldglasses as a pair of cubs—they must have been eating wild meat—squared off and the larger of the two jumped the other and slashed at it with such fury that it looked as if the smaller cub might be killed. The mother studied the fighters only a moment, then waded into the battle, cuffed the raging youngsters apart and proceeded to lambaste the aggressor until it came fawning at her feet with all four paws waving in the air as it begged forgiveness.

Ralph Young frankly admits that the more he sees of brownies and grizzlies, the more puzzled he is at their vagaries. He says this is especially true of mothers and cubs. Biologists say that the female should normally give birth to a single cub in the third year of her life, and every other year thereafter she should produce a litter of from one to four. The cubs are supposed to den with the mother during their first winter, but start foraging for themselves when mama again becomes a June bride in the following summer. Ralph knows what the book says; he also knows what he sees.

"Once I saw a sow-bear with five cubs trailing her. Only two looked like her own, so where did the other three come from? Another day I saw six grizzlies in a traveling band: two sows and four cubs all mingling in one happy family. By way of contrast, I witnessed a sow with one cub fighting another sow with two cubs. The winner left with all three cubs. The loser turned around and went the other way."

The point Ralph makes over and over again is this: There isn't a year when he doesn't see a grizzly break all the known rules of behavior by doing something entirely different.

"On numerous occasions I've met up with a sow-bear who had cubs bigger than she was, though in every instance mama was boss," says Young. "Then there was the female who, instead of giving birth to her cubs in winter hibernation like she was supposed to, must have gone to den with a boar and bedded down all winter with him, because her cubs weren't born until the following summer!"

There was nothing unusual about the female bear who attacked a schoolteacher near Juneau a few years ago, though the manner of his escape was by no means routine. He was hiking along a mountain goat trail to a high trout stream when he saw a mother grizzly stripping salmonberries below the trail. On the high side he heard snuffling noises and whines indicating cubs, and he realized immediately that he was in for an exciting afternoon. He had been told that from the time the tiny, naked babes are born to her until she weds again almost two years later, all the cubs have to do is squeal for help and mama becomes a snarling buzz saw. That's what happened this day. The cubs let out yowls of alarm, the mother chuffed, and suddenly the schoolteacher remembered what an old-timer had told him to do under such circumstances. Whistle! Putting fingers to lips the teacher shrilled with tremolo effects he hadn't intended. Only the fact that the bear had to come uphill to get him saved his life.

As the salmonberry briars exploded, the schoolteacher streaked for the nearest spruce, leaped for a limb and was hauling himself to safety when the bear nipped his boot heel and began yanking furiously. "She had me waving out there like a flag in the breeze," said the teacher that night, teeth still chattering from the ordeal. "She stretched my backbone like an accordion. But I hung on."

This desperate tug-of-war went on for some time. "Finally," said the teacher, "a strap broke and the boot came off. Either that, or she'd have pulled a leg off. I know doggone well my arms weren't letting go."

After giving the boot a thorough drubbing as an example of what might have happened, the mother bear gathered up her cubs and departed, and the schoolteacher was left with a tale that would make him suspect as a liar for the rest of his life.

9   The Deadlier Female

But another Juneau resident, and this one a highly skilled woodsman, could not escape the deadly rage of a female bear. During my twenty-five years in Alaska, many of them as head of its wildlife department, I had spent a lot of time in grizzly country with the victim. Of all the sportsmen I knew up there, I would rate Rod Darnell close to the top in knowing how to protect himself in the forest. His nerves were steady, his eyes quick, and he was a deadly rifle shot. In spite of his skills, a grizzly got him, and if it could happen to Rod Darnell it could happen to anybody. That's why I have selected his savage mauling as a case example.

It happened on a gloomy morning in September. The mountain peaks of Chichagof Island, a few miles west of Juneau, were lost in fog, and shreds of mist clung to the giant hemlocks and spruces on the lower slopes. With packboard on his back Darnell pushed through the chilly gray shadows of the deep timber along a trail he himself had kept blazed through the years. Hunting companions Vern Clemons and Ree Reindeau followed, alert for the sight of the small Sitka bucks they were after.

Two hundred yards in from the shoreline, Darnell swung around a brush patch to the first open muskeg, and in that moment disaster struck. There wasn't any warning. Right in front of Rod were three grizzly bears, usually known as brownies to Alaskans. Two of the beasts, later determined to be oversize yearling cubs, snorted as they crashed out of sight in the jungle of tangled evergreens and devil's-club. They didn't go very far, because Darnell said he could still hear them moaning and huffing. But it was the third bear that told Rod he was in trouble. Not twenty paces away, it had swung around to face him, its heavy black lips wrinkled back to show its fangs.

"The slung rifle came sliding off my shoulder," recalled Darnell as he lay in the hospital days later. "I yanked the bolt to jack a cartridge into the firing chamber. I heard my voice sounding a warning to Vern and Ree. But they were too far back to spot the bears. They had no way of knowing, until it was too late, that I'd run into a killer."

Darnell said the grizzly turned her head away for a brief moment, her eyes following her yearling cubs, hustling them into hiding with rapidly ejaculated throaty sounds. He hoped that during this short space of time the female might decide to follow her young ones out of sight; that having covered their retreat, she, too would make a getaway.

It was a vain hope. This female was not going to run away. She was going to attack. Rod remembers her eyes burning with greenish glare through the fog and foam bubbling from her open jaws. Vern and Ree, he said, were just coming around an alder clump when the maddened mother buttoned her ears flat against the broad skull and came roaring into her charge.

Darnell described the wide-open mouth and the flying slobber as the she-bear closed the gap between them with incredible speed. He had realized in a flash there would be time only for one shot and that it would have to be snapped without aiming. The blazing eyes of the beast were exactly level with his own, he noted, as the bear came on in a head-high rush. And somehow, in the split-second interval before she hit, the thought raced through his mind that one swipe from the great paw of this beast could break his head loose from his body. For him, this could be like a lightning stroke.

Where the 220-grain bullet from his .30-06 rifle hit, he never knew. Rod pulled the trigger, and then instantaneously did the thing that was to save his life. He pivoted away from the rushing monster, dove headfirst into the spongy muskeg, and clamped both arms around the back of his head and neck. Instantly, the massive bulk was on him like a huge, savage dog, fangs slashing for the vulnerable spot where spine and skull came together. The she-devil meant to finish him off in a hurry.

"Strangely," said Darnell, "I have no recollection of being hurt as the bear's teeth bit into my arm and all but tore it loose at the socket as she flung it out of her way." Moving with speed faster than any human could ever match, the raging female crushed her long fangs into his shoulder, lifted him clear and whacked him against the muskeg. "And still," insisted Darnell, "there was no sensation of pain."

He didn't know how to explain it; maybe it was shock. He seemed to be fully conscious as he fought for his life in the only way that he stood a chance; letting himself go limp but managing to twist about so he always landed stomach down with his hands clasped around the nape of his neck. He remembers seeing a hand fly past his eyes, gushing blood like a leaky hose, and he flung it back again as he rooted desperately into the damp sphagnum moss.

Rod Darnell had spent a lifetime among these Alaska grizzlies. He'd been taught that, above all, he must not attempt to fight off one of these huge beasts with his bare hands. He must not permit it to flip him over belly up where it could rake out his guts with a single scoop of its meathook claws. His only chance was to make the bear believe it had killed him; to feign death and at the same time try to shield his vital parts. Though he realized he might pass out like a light at any time, Darnell said he felt an odd sort of detachment, like he was being spun in a vacuum—almost as if this macabre thing were happening to someone else. But that was before the grizzly took his entire head into her mouth and attempted to crush it.

She had been pushing Rod farther into the wet muskeg, her jaws pressing hard against the back of his skull, all the while screaming her rage and frustration. Then, suddenly, her teeth clamped together with paralyzing force, and Rod was flung into the air and thrashed about like a rag doll shaken by a terrier. He fully expected his neck to snap and he was helpless to do anything to prevent it. But even worse tortures were to come. When it appeared he had been mauled beyond any hope of recovery, all at once he felt excruciating agony. It was not from the grizzly's teeth gripping his head, but in the chest bone. The cartilage had been ripped loose from the bone, and the cause of it was a pair of binoculars hung over his neck and now hammering the very life out of his lungs as the she-brute flailed his body against the ground to end it all.

"It seemed to me I'd already taken more punishment than a man could recover from," Darnell told me, and he thought his time was up. "Suddenly, in a dizzy popping of stars, there came a violent explosion. Everything seemed to let go. My head was flung from the bear's mouth."

When Rod opened his eyes, all he could see at first was red. "My hands looked like paintbrushes dipped in crimson. Blood was streaming down my face. It welled and bubbled from my

shoulders and neck and chest." His companions said Rod was
sprawled like a broken thing among uprooted clods of moss
and meadow grass, drenched in his own gore. The place was
like a slaughter pen, they said, and they had little hope that he
would survive. The foggy air was foul with animal stench.
Right alongside the stricken hunter the brown, blood-smeared
hulk of the killer grizzly heaved in horrid, dying convulsions.

"I managed to raise myself on one elbow just as Ree shoved
the muzzle of his rifle against the grizzly's head and pulled the
trigger," explained Darnell. "There was a blast of red spray
against my face. Then came a shudder and a long sigh. The
she-devil was dead."

Vern Clemons, who had saved his life a few seconds before
by shooting the beast off his body, now dropped to his knees,
and Rod could read the horror of his appearance mirrored in
his friend's eyes. It had been Clemons' first Alaska deer hunt
and Darnell said he had turned it into a nightmare for him.
He'd planned to show Vern and Ree his secretly-blazed trail
leading to a horseshoe-shaped meadow at timberline where the
blacktail bucks fed themselves hog-fat in the fall. It was the
venison that Vern wanted, not a dying man on his hands.

"We all put on a show of being cheerful," said Rod as he
recalled the awful moments. "They'd have me patched and
back on the deer hunt right away. I went along with the decep-
tion, though none of us were fooling anybody. I knew my
chances were on the slim side. We were seventy miles from
Juneau by water, and two hundred yards inland from the uninhabited shores of Whitestone Harbor where we'd dragged
a skiff and an outboard motor to the high-tide line. Out in the
bay, riding at anchor, was my gas boat *Liability*. That I could
survive the ocean trip after being put aboard the gas boat
appeared doubtful. We'd have to get lucky."

The flour sacks were the first good break. They'd been
brought along in the packboards to wrap up the dressed ven-

ison. Vern and Ree tore them apart and bound the strips around Rod's neck, shoulders and upper part of the chest, putting on strong pressure to stop the bleeding that otherwise would have drained his life away on the spot. There wasn't much they could do with his lacerated scalp except to plaster back a flap of skin and hair which had been peeled off by the bear's teeth and which hung down like an earflap. And while they trussed him up mummy-style, Rod made a hopeful discovery.

The stiff packboard had protected his back from serious harm, so that the bear had confined most of its butchering to the upper section of his body. It hadn't slashed into him below the hips. When Vern and Ree carefully hoisted him to his feet, Rod found he could hobble and that he wasn't a stretcher case yet. But he knew he was a long way from being out of the woods. In spite of the tight bandages, wrapped layer upon layer, blood continued to seep through at an alarming rate.

The effort of groping down to the skiff at the water's edge opened Darnell's wounds again. The nylon parka hood folded down at the back of his neck had become a big bubble full of blood. His companions realized he would be bled white if he didn't get surgical care without delay. Rod began to experience low periods, and he told Vern and Ree not to attempt the 70-mile voyage to Juneau through choppy seas but to head directly across Chatham Straits to the Funter Bay salmon cannery where they could radio-phone for a plane and a doctor. There appeared small chance of meeting another vessel on the way, but if they saw one with radio transmitter they should try to head it off. Giddy spells were warning Rod that he might black out at any moment.

For Darnell if for nobody else, the mail boat *Forrester* was exactly on schedule that Saturday morning of September 29, 1957. At the hail from the gas boat *Liability*, Captain Don Gallagher drifted alongside to hear their S O S message and had it on the air before the three deer hunters were under way to Funter Bay again. Vern and Ree had barely enough time to moor the *Liability* at the cannery float when a two-motored Grumann amphibian plane roared overhead, banked sharply, and landed with a splash. It came racing in on the step, and the next thing Rod Darnell realized he was airborne and Dr. Rude was examining his awful wounds. Minutes later he was in the hospital in Juneau. Just before he went under the anesthetic someone told him that only one hour and forty minutes had elapsed since Vern Clemon's rifle-shot at point blank range had blasted the crazed she-bear off his body.

It took the doctor and nurses the rest of the day to clean and sew Darnell's wounds together and start the blood transfusions that pulled him through. Four hours on the operating table, weeks of painful convalescence and rebandaging, scarred for a lifetime! And how long had it taken the bear to inflict the damage? It had seemed like an hour to Darnell. He said he would not have believed the actual time except that Vern and Ree agreed on it. "No more than thirty seconds," they told him. At that rate he could not possibly have survived a full minute under the grizzly's teeth and claws.

Few men have even been closer to death and lived to tell about it than Rod Darnell. His philosophy on the subject therefore attains a value not possible in the mere theorist. Three times in previous years, Rod had faced savage grizzlies and each time managed to talk them out of charging by speaking to them as one would talk to an angry dog threatening to bite. He'd never wanted to kill a bear. In all his life he had never gone bear hunting. The big beasts had nothing to fear from Darnell. He said he wished there were some way of letting them know it.

"I've always figured the big bears were entitled to their place in the wildlife picture, and an asset to Alaska," he reasoned. "If there are guides and nonresidents who want to hunt them for trophies, they're welcome to my share. Most of us who live in Alaska feel the same way. We'd like to live and let live. But how are we going to make this known to the bears?"

It was a good question. The bears would like to know, too.

q What Makes a Grizzly Attack

Most woodsmen who have shared the trails with grizzly bears for a few years are in general agreement that about one bear out of twenty-five will face up to a man and perhaps charge him. Possibly half of the attacks will be by distraught mothers defending their cubs. Some will be from wounded bears fighting for their lives. Other attacks will come from bears protecting a food cache; some by bears mistaking a human for a natural enemy like another bear. There will be still other cases beyond the ability of any man to figure out.

There was Hans, fisherman from the "old country," who left his salmon-troller anchored near my powerlaunch in Lisianski Straits and climbed a forested ridge from shoreline to timberline to shoot a deer for his mulligan pot. Hours later, with darkness coming on, I heard Hans shouting for help, and rowed a skiff to shore just in time to see him dragging himself down a game trail. His clothes were blood-soaked, his gun

was gone, and he had wrapped two sticks around his left leg
to splint a fracture.

After I had him aboard his boat and had performed first
aid, Hans told me he didn't know how it happened. He hadn't
heard a sound or seen a move. His first warning had been the
body of the bear sailing toward him out of the brush. The
grizzly had belted him unconscious and then gone on its way.
When Hans came to he said he looked around for the bear and
for his rifle. He couldn't find either one. Adding to the mystery,
Hans hadn't the foggiest notion why the bear had jumped
him. "Ay yoost minding my own business up dere," he
shrugged.

I'm not sure I have any better explanation for what had
happened on my own first deer hunt several years earlier. Anyway, I'll take the blame for what took place the day Indian
Sumdum Charlie initiated me in the art of shooting blacktail
bucks near Kootznahoo, Home of the Bears. We anchored
the little gas boat in Bear Cove and sculled ashore. We dragged
the skiff across empty clam shells and squishy kelp bulbs to
high-tide line, looped the painter around a barnacled rock,
and started into the big timber. Sumdum Charlie swung onto
a grizzly trail and I followed the puffing, heavy-set Tlingit
Indian through a mist-hung forest until we came to a patch
of open muskeg.

Still in the gray gloom of the giant evergreens, Sumdum
lowered his ample rump onto a downed cedar. "No more
walk," he grunted. "No more talk. Plenty mowitch this place."

From a sealskin scabbard, Indian Charlie pulled a homemade knife made out of an old file and began whittling. When
he had finished, he had himself a thin shaving of green buck-
brush clamped between two small concave cedar blocks. And
when Sumdum Charlie held this whittled instrument to his
fat lips and his brown cheeks puffed out like the full moon,
you could almost smell venison chops sizzling in the skillet.

When Sumdum played his deer call the music that came forth was something the small Sitka bucks couldn't resist; three soft, wheezy little notes, something like breathing across a grass blade held between the thumbs. Wait five minutes, then do it again.

Sometimes, whispered Sumdum Charlie, there'd be no need to make the second series of calls. This was one of those days. At first, I saw nothing; only hefty Charlie humped like a Buddha, his head slowly swiveling toward the left. Very slowly he put aside the cedar blocks and eased a rust-eaten old .45-90 trade rifle to his shoulder. It was then that I made out a fan ear cocked behind a stunted jack pine, and a three-forked antler. At the booming whump of the rifle they slumped out of sight.

Sumdum mixed grunts and groans as he dragged the buck to our stand and spread-eagled the carcass across the log to drain. "Plenty more this place," came his guttural whisper as he handed me the magic blocks. "You call own mowitch."

Somehow, the wheezes I produced seemed to suggest not romance but asthma. After a quarter hour of rasping squeaks wafted across the muskeg, the only game in sight was a speckled fawn. Its eyes were bugged out far enough to knock off with a stick as it stared entranced, paying no heed to the warnings of an excited doe stamping her dainty hoofs in the forest dark. A red chickaree squirrel started flicking its plume on a limb and scolding vigorously. This started a chain reaction among the blue Steller's paybirds and chicadees, punctuated at intervals by the doleful *kabloonk* of a raven. Still hopeful, I waited five minutes, then sent out three more quavering mating calls. I haven't blown a deer call since. Because that was the moment when 900 pounds of trouble came roaring down upon my friend Sumdum Charlie and me.

Sumdum is good enough to say I shouldn't take all the blame. The big Indian says he thinks the smell of the gutted buck on the cedar log had plenty to do with what happened.

The spotted fawn, almost in our laps when I heard its answering bleat for the last time, didn't help us any; neither did the scolding squirrel and the shrieking jays. The smell and the racket were bound to attract attention from the shaggy boss of these woods. The eerie croak of the raven might have been meant as a warning.

When the grizzly exploded out of the devil's club I dropped the deer call and grabbed for my rifle. This bear meant trouble. It wasn't bluffing. There wasn't any show of teeth-popping or other kinds of scare tactics. It had marked us down cold and was coming in a direct, silent charge. I remember the green glare in its small eyes, the blood gushing from its mouth as it fell back on its haunches. Sumdum Charlie's relic .45-90 blasted my eardrums. The bear was down to rise no more.

Charlie still thinks it must have been the fresh-killed buck and not the deer call that caused the grizzly to stalk and attack. Sumdum says it wanted the meat. I'm not saying, because what that bear had in mind neither Sumdum Charlie nor I can ever be sure. Only the grizzly knew.

But when able bear-men like Admiralty Island's Ed Jahncke and full-whiskered Allen Hasselborg of Mole Harbor get mauled, it's because they are taking calculated risks to recover grizzlies already wounded. They know the hurt beast will plunge into the densest cover if it can, and that it will almost surely circle back to ambush the man on its blood trail.

Guide Ed Jahncke knew all this from long experience, yet, because the grizzly was an outstanding trophy wounded by one of his hunter clients, and because he felt an obligation to end the beast's suffering, he shoved cautiously into the blueberry brush, step at a time, rifle ready for a quick shot at close range. He said he had his first inkling of the peril involved when he came to a knoll and saw splatters of gore leading straight up the steepest part. He said he knew then that the bear had not been critically weakened or it would have gone around the bottom of the hill. He saw red drops on the fallen spruce needles leading around an uprooted windfall. He eased ahead a few short steps, then set himself for fast action.

"And still I wasn't quick enough," he told me afterward. "The thing was on me in a flash." Suddenly, Jahncke was knocked flat, then gripped in enormous jaws and flailed against the ground with deadly purpose. "I thought I was a goner," said Ed. "I would have been, too, if the man I was guiding had stayed back in the clear as I told him to." Instead, the hunter had followed close behind the guide as he trailed the wounded grizzly, and was on hand to finish the job.

The other guide, the aforementioned and famous Allen Hasselborg, was collecting bear specimens for Dr. C. Hart Merriam of the old U.S. Bureau of Biological Survey back in 1912, when a grizzly he had wounded jumped on him from a ledge. Its teeth fastened into Hasselborg's right arm and he was dragged along the snow-covered ground. Realizing his only chance was to feign death, Hasselborg let himself go limp. This was made all the more convincing to the grizzly when the entire sleeve of his heavy wool jacket ripped loose at the shoulder. Flinging it aside, the grizzly left him, and Hasselborg had the fortitude to bear the excruciating pain of shredded arm muscles, to play dead until the grizzly was out of sight.

Sometimes, the thinnest hairline may separate the roaring attack of a grizzly from merely a bad scare. The whole drama may hinge on an unpredictable turning point over which man has no control; like what happened the summer I helped Hank Lucas count moose on Kenai Peninsula.

Hank was asleep in the July sunshine and it was my turn to glass the willow-grown slopes. I'd tallied five great bulls, their heavy antlers clubby in velvet, and seven raggedly-shedding cows with eight chocolate-colored calves. As my binoculars swept the high country toward the head of Tustumena Glacier they ringed a yellow sow-bear with twin cubs. We'd already had a run-in with this cantankerous old girl, but now she was ambling for a divide above timberline, and I guessed we'd have no more trouble with her for a few days at least. What I didn't know was that another grizzly was crouched in some alders working up a real mad less than a stone's toss away.

From Hank's cabin on Skilak Lake we'd been making leg trips across the willow plateaus, backpacking our grub and bedding, snatching a few hours' rest whenever we had a chance. We had no more schedule than a jackrabbit. We'd been siwashing under the open sky so long that we were brown as Indians, stubble-faced as a couple of Airedales, pinch-gutted as coyotes; and because we never knew what minute we'd bust head on into a sour-tempered grizzly we'd developed jumpy nerves. When we picked a spot to rest we favored open places like the mossy bank of Funny River, where we'd settled down that July noon.

One at a time we bellied down on the gravel for a pull of ice water, our eyes no more than a dozen feet from a pair of hooknosed king salmon threshing out a spawning redd in the rubble. A school of red-spotted Dolly Varden trout darted around, snapping up the pea-sized pink roe that floated away. The bar was churned with moose hoofs; a pair of ravens hopped away from the skeleton of a bear-killed salmon, and Hank pointed in silence to a grizzly pad print in which the water was still roily. He wiped his mouth with his sleeve as he climbed up the bank and settled down against his packsack while I uncased the binoculars and got out my tally sheet. Before Hank let his eyes fall shut he took a long, careful look all around us.

The first warning I got wasn't very much, just a low moaning in the alder patch. I could barely hear it. I'd heard porcupines do better. I looked at Hank, sleeping with our only gun across his knees and decided not to disturb him. And then I saw that his eyes were wide open and his left hand reaching for his rifle. Without a word he worked the bolt and a cartridge clicked home in the firing chamber.

The moans stopped abruptly and there was only an ominous stillness in the thicket. All at once I felt prickly at the back of my neck. This was close quarters. Hank eased the butt of his .30-06 to his shoulder but nothing stirred. A couple of minutes passed, and then Hank wet a forefinger and held it up to the wind. Motioning for me to follow, he angled away until our scent carried straight across the alder patch. Whispered the guide, "This will smoke him out."

Through the green leaves I caught a glimpse of blurred gunny-sack brown. Hank's rifle pointed but did not fire. The bear seemed to be fading back, the brush tops trembling to mark its course. We followed its movements to the far edge of the alders and then we saw it clear; a great dish-faced brute swinging its enormous head and skinning its lips. With shoulder hackles on edge it stalked stiffly over a low hilltop and out of sight.

I took a deep breath. "Good way to get rid of a grizzly," I said.

Hank was still holding his rifle at ready. "Don't be too sure," he grunted. "Sometimes the man-smell starts trouble in a hurry. You have to gamble." He nodded toward the big king salmon pounding the pool into foam with their egg-laying. "The grizzly wants those salmon. It might come back." ·

When it did, I thought, we would be long gone. As soon as we finished the evening count of moose we'd be on our way across the high ridges to the Killey River lick for another day of spotting. Hank planned to show me a sampling of the entire summer range between Skilak and Tustumena Lakes, which meant at least another hundred miles of backpacking. He knew the Kenai Peninsula wilderness the way a farmer knows his cow pastures, and he knew the animals almost as well. The common black bears were everywhere. Sometimes we'd spot fifteen or twenty grubbing on the carpets of lingonberries, paying us no mind as we walked within a few yards. Hank offered to bet me he could get close enough to spank one on the behind with the flat of his hand.

But the lean little guide didn't horse around with the yellow grizzlies. There seemed to be two species on the Kenai, and they were both resentful of humans. One was a large brownie known as the Kenai giant bear, and the other was the Alexander grizzly, largest of the continent grizzlies since California wiped out its great golden bear. Any time Hank saw either kind he gave it a wide berth. He never plowed into a thicket without first scanning the edges for fresh bear sign.

In late afternoon after our second meal of the day, Hank pulled the skillet off the dying embers and slicked it clean with a handful of sphagnum moss. This was the sunset hour when the moose came out in the open glades to fill their paunches, and it was a sight to see! There had been no more than two dozen in view during the middle of the day, but the slanting red sunrays on their backs revealed moose in every direction. Our count zoomed to a total of eighty-seven, every one of them within easy stalking range.

I pointed to an exceptionally tall, dark bull with huge flat antlers that promised to develop into a record-breaking set come the fall rutting season in September. But Hank wasn't paying any attention—not to me. He'd turned his head to eye the alder patch behind us. Said the guide quietly, "That bear is here again."

I stole a look at the riffle in Funny River to see if the salmon were still there. They were floundering aimlessly about; they'd finished spawning and now they were only a pair of battered red hulks waiting for death that comes to all Pacific salmon at such time. If the bear wants them, I thought, he's welcome to have them.

Again the low moans reached our ears, ominous and persistent. A yellow head came pushing into view. Hank froze in his tracks and talked quite normally to it. "Go back. Get out

of here." The reply was a belly-deep *whuff*, followed by rapid
clicking of teeth.

The giant bear seemed to rise two feet higher on its four
stiffened legs as it advanced toward us along a curving trail
leading past the dying embers of our campfire and down into
the river. I knew without Hank's saying that if the pads of the
bear deviated from this trail he would shoot. It would be very
close, no more than fifteen yards, time enough for only one
shot.

My eyes dropped and riveted on the turn in the trail. This
was the spot! Then I couldn't see the trail any more because
it was hidden by two paws. Time stood still as the paws
stopped. Still Hank didn't fire.

A forepaw lifted off the ground and hung poised, then it
swung left and the next thing I saw were two hind feet moving
away. A stern end like a haystack disappeared over the river
bank, and right afterward was a watery explosion as the
grizzly plunged in to claim his bounty.

"Let's get the hell out of here," I heard Hank say. But he
wasn't talking to me. I was already on my way.

q The Brown Bandits

In Alaska, where the grizzly's favorite summer food, salmon, is not available it will turn to the mammal life around it. Let the grizzly find a mountain meadow honeycombed with the shallow push-ups of voles and lemmings and it will rake out and gobble down the plump little rodents like a chicken scratching for corn. The bigger ground squirrels and marmots require a little more digging. For red meat in still larger packages, like deer, elk, mountain sheep, caribou, and moose, the brown bandit may have to spend hours, perhaps days, to make a killing. It will sneak on its belly for long distances, taking advantage of every dip and cover, to finally close with a tremendous burst of speed.

Andy Simons is not one to discount the eyesight of an open-country grizzly, though there is much talk about nearsightedness among bears. Andy has observed that while bears may not see sharply toward their rear or side, there is nothing weak about their straight-ahead vision. Andy notes, that like other predators, the bear's eyes are deep-set in the front of their skulls. When we were together, I noted that Simons took some liberties with bears facing away or in profile to us, but froze motionless when the grizzly turned full face.

Even so, when pitted against an alert prey whose prominent eyes are placed more to the side of the head to pick up lateral or rear movement, the grizzly rarely catches up with any but weakened or very young game animals. It is far more adept at smelling out game already dead from natural causes—the riper the better—or making off with carcasses taken by hunters. In this the bears show extraordinary strength and audacity.

A gold prospector, name of Joe Nelson, in the Crazy Hills north of Fairbanks, shot a fat bull caribou one August day, hauled the 300-pound carcass down to his cabin and hoisted it free of the ground on a crossbar between two trees. Next morning it was gone, though not without a trace. Joe could plainly see where his winter meat supply had been dragged away. The trail led up a gully over one mountaintop, down on the other side, up an almost perpendicular slope, and finally into a dense thicket of white birches where prospector Joe knew better than to follow. "It was a lot safer," he told me later over a cup of coffee, "to shoot me another caribou."

In the same central Alaska region, a popular guide of a few years ago, John Hajdukovich, had the consistent good luck of sending his clients back to their clubs in the big cities with exciting motion pictures climaxed by a charging grizzly. John's secret, which he guarded for several years, was based on intimate study of the fierce Toklat grizzly—by nature and circumstance an aggressive flesh-eater—and by John's bullfighter tactics. As soon as they killed the first trophy of the hunt and removed antlers and cape and camp meat, Hajdukovich would build a brush blind *downwind* from the remains, and at the earliest evidence of a grizzly in the vicinity he would assemble the hunting party around the blind.

"We let the bear get a good taste of the meat," explained Hajdukovich, "then I show myself just a little, maybe wave my hat above the bush tops, and I grunt like another bear."

The grizzly's instinctive action was to put on a furious charge to bluff the interloper away. That is when the hidden cameraman started turning the crank, with instructions to keep grinding away no matter how close the bear came. At point blank range, when the viewfinder was all brown fur, John and his two helpers would leap to their feet and confront the grizzly. While the helpers held rifles at ready, John would contribute the crowning touch by flinging his jacket in the bear's face and dodging away like a toreador.

"It wasn't really dangerous," insisted Hajdukovich. "Sometimes we didn't have to shoot the bear." In a questionnaire addressed to the nation's leading bear hunters some years ago, FIELD & STREAM Magazine asked: *Will a grizzly bear attack without being provoked?* John Hajdukovich answered, "Yes." But he didn't define his idea of provocation.

A not so well-known trait of the big brownies and grizzlies is their tendency to cannibalism. The skinned carcass of a trophy bear left in the field is almost sure to be reduced to bones by other bears. There are numerous incidents involving cubs killed and devoured by the old males, and there have been examples of adult boars fighting duels to death, with the victors eating their fill of the losers. A bear surprised by a man while it is munching grass or gathering wild berries is not likely to display such ferocity as another bear standing guard over a cache of meat. Many veteran bear-men think this is a grizzly at its most dangerous time. Ray Deardorf, Juneau mining engineer, found this out one frosty morning in the nearby Taku River Valley.

On the evening before Deardorf had shot a bull moose and had time only to open it up and remove the viscera before darkness closed in and he had to hurry to a tent camp on the bank of the Taku River which he shared with a fellow engineer. At break of day he started back to the moose kill with butcher knife, meat saw, and packboard for relaying out the several hundred pounds of venison. Ray was crossing an open patch of muskeg almost within sight of his downed bull when the bushes parted to frame the broad yellow head of a very large grizzly.

Said Deardorf, "I knew what it meant. I hadn't brought a rifle with me, so it meant I'd have to climb a tree. But I wasn't too badly alarmed. There was a spruce tree with limbs spaced just right for scaling no more than two jumps away."

But it wasn't near enough and Deardof was caught and savagely drubbed.

The giant grizzly that mauled Ray Deardorf is believed to be the same beast who tried to muscle in on my old friend Oscar Olson, Taku River homesteader. The facts were revealed to me under unusual circumstances during the following summer when I accompanied a young game warden on a river-boat patrol to investigate a reported out-of-season moose killing. In front of old-timer Oscar's log cabin, we ran the shovel nose of our long river boat up on a sandbar, and game warden Duggie stepped ashore to be greeted with a murderous howling of sled dogs and rattling of heavy chains. There was an earthy roar from Oscar, loaded with Scandinavian accent. I climbed the bank to see the towering figure of Oscar advancing threateningly on young Duggie. The big Norwegian spotted me and his manner changed. We were old acquaintances, and this was why I had made the long trip down from Juneau with the newly-appointed warden. The violation report filed against homesteader Oscar just didn't square with my estimate of the man.

A stentorian bellow from the old loner sent his sled dogs cringing into their individual kennels to which their chains were stapled. We walked the narrow footpath gingerly to the cabin door and felt the puncheon floor beneath our rubber boot soles. Oscar had been eating breakfast when his dogs sounded the alarm. Now, he covered the greased griddle top with some more sourdough batter, poked a couple of white birch sticks into the firebox, and poured us each a mug of stout coffee.

Right away I sensed that something was wrong. Generally garrulous as a neighborhood gossip over the backyard fence, Oscar wasn't talking this morning. With pancake turner in hand he squinted down at us, his shaggy hair nearly brushing the pole ceiling, his shoulders two axe-handles wide. He looked skookum enough to drag a whale sideways through the woods.

As Duggie flooded burnt-sugar syrup over his flapjacks the wheels of his young mind milled on the job he had come to do. He had to find out if or why big Oscar had violated the law, and Oscar's silence was ominous.

A complaint had reached the Juneau office of the old Alaska Game Commission. Rifle firing had been reported by an up-river neighbor with whom Oscar had been mildly feuding for the past twenty ears. A cow moose had been seen to plunge down over the sandbank at Oscar's place and go crashing into the river. Later, the inquisitive neighbor had sneaked a look into Oscar's smokehouse and had seen fresh quarters of meat hanging in the alder smoke.

Choosing the direct approach as suggested in the manual, young Duggie proceeded to lay all his information on the table. Big Oscar listened, his blue eyes unwavering, and when the officer finished, the burly homesteader dropped a mighty paw on his shoulder. "Coom now," he rumbled, "ve geev a luke."

There were rows of slabbed red-fleshed salmon hanging from the cross-poles in the smokehouse, but no game meat.

As he was thoughtfully wending his way back to Oscar's cabin to drink some more coffee over this unexpected development, Duggie gave a sudden start. Why not go see the complaining neighbor? Here, too, he drew a blank. The neighbor had now suffered a change of heart, fearing Oscar's wrath. By the time we returned to his cabin to spend the night, the sun was down and the stage set for another strange bit of action.

It came with the rising of the Taku wind during the night. As we sat at breakfast next morning, ready to leave for town within the hour, Duggie's glance fell on an oddly moving object. It was a rope's frayed end whipping in the early sunlight. When the breeze died away the rope fell back against the shadow-darkened trunk of a spruce tree to remain invisible until another gust tossed it clear again. After breakfast Duggie sauntered casually to the big spruce, looked upward and beckoned to me. Behind me I was aware of the soft thumping of Oscar's No. 12 boots.

Well up in the gloom of thickly growing branches a pulley block had been fastened, and beneath it were swinging several bulky objects. Duggie lowered them to the ground. They were chunks of fresh meat. They had been sprinkled with black pepper and had hung in the smoke somewhere long enough to form a hard crust. The disclosure more or less backed up the complaint lodged by Oscar's unfriendly neighbor, though there was a minor discrepancy. This was not moose meat, I told Duggie; it was grizzly bear.

The young warden was only temporarily taken back. Moose or grizzly, it was still against the Alaska Game Law regulations to kill big game in the summer. Oscar's only line of defense was to claim and offer reasonable proof that the bear had been about to attack him when he shot. The fact that Oscar had concealed the meat indicated guilt; until he explained that the meat had been hoisted high enough to keep it clear of bluebottle blow-flies.

Duggie framed his next question carefully, aware that his case against the homesteader hung in the balance. "Did the bear charge you?" he asked.

Oscar pondered the query, his pale blue eyes shining with candor. "Ay don't vait to see. Ay yoost shoot."

Having in my own time met up with a few of these cantankerous Taku grizzlies and with the vicious attacks on Ray Deardorf and Rod Darnell in mind, I was inclined to waive all further questioning. But young Duggie's zeal was such as to insist that Oscar show us where and how it had happened.

The three of us trudged down to the landing, Oscar cranked up the engine in his fish scow, and we started upriver to where the corks from Oscar's gill net trailed in an eddy. The sandbar was punched deep with bear tracks the diameter of a man's hat. Oscar laid his big hands to the net and walked it out on the bar high and dry. The webbing looked as if it had been chopped up with an axe.

"Bears?" questioned Duggie.

"No," said Oscar firmly. "Yoost vun bear."

And then he told us about the grizzly that had started robbing his net, finally getting to the point where it was pulling it out of the water and ripping the fish out of it, leaving none for Oscar. Even worse, when the homesteader showed up, the grizzly met him at the bank and chased him back into his scow.

To agent Duggie it must have been clear that Oscar's killing of the grizzly had not been without legal justification, but he insisted on having the rest of the facts, and Oscar obliged. The day it happened, said Oscar, he arrived at the sandbar to find neither bear nor gill net; only a trail of torn-up bushes leading up the hill. When Oscar caught up with the grizzly it had one of the cork floats in its jaws and was backing uphill with furious energy. Puffing and grunting, it was dragging the net full of flopping salmon into the woods.

At the sight of such bold skullduggery, Oscar said he lost his head. It was the only net he had and he needed it to finish putting up enough dried salmon to last him and his sled dogs all winter. He said he grabbed onto the trailing end of the webbing, shook his rifle in the air, and yelled loudly for the bear to let loose.

"Did it?" questioned Duggie sharply.

"So qvick ay don't believe it," retorted the old homesteader. He said the grizzly dropped the cork from its teeth, roared like a mad bull, and started down the trail after him.

Duggie had heard enough to satisfy the law. "That," he admitted, "is what I call a real attack."

Oscar looked at me with his honest blue eyes, and I imagined for a moment that the left eyelid drooped slightly. "Vell," he told the young game warden, "ay von't tell no lie. Ay don't vait to see. Ay yoost shoot."

⟨ Babes and Yearlings

One May day while guiding a hunter on Alaska Peninsula where the Aleutian Islands begin, Andy Simons was glassing the snow-covered crags when he spotted a rare sight. It was a she-bear in the very act of breaking through the snow as she came out of her winter den. Ringed in his binoculars a snowdrift came pushing up, split into petals like those of an unfolding daisy, and out of the center into the bright sunlight came the yellow head of a Peninsula super grizzly.

Andy tapped his hunter on the knee and they were both focused on the spot when the female reached back into the hole and lifted out a tiny cub in her teeth. The little fellow, hardly larger than a cat, hunched shivering in the first snow it had ever felt, terrified at the sudden daylight. When the she-bear turned around to drag out another cub, the first one scuttled back into the burrow.

The mother kept pulling them out, said Andy, and they kept diving back until she found a way to end it. She plodded some distance from the den entrance and slumped comfortably back against a soft snowbank like a plump lady in a rocking chair. Torn between the dark security of the cave—the only home they'd known in their four months of life—and the warm comfort of the mother and her inviting nipples, the cubs made their choice and were soon snuggling in the fur of the she-bear's breast.

After she had fed them, the mother started guiding her family slowly away from the den toward the blue ocean far in the distance, the youngsters quickly adapting themselves to the dazzling snowscape before them, eager to learn more about it. The route led along a snow cornice overhanging several hundred feet of sheer space. One cub scampered to the edge, suddenly recoiled in fright and ran all the way back to hide under the mother's belly, peeking timidly out through a curtain of long hair. Then it was the second baby's turn and he was made of sterner stuff. Crawling to the rim, he stretched his neck full length to peer over the dropoff. It fascinated him, and soon he was joined by the other cub. Side by side they hung head down, gazing spellbound at the vast new world below.

Farther down from the pinnacles the she-bear took her ease on an exposed flat rock while the cubs wrestled and played tag. They found a wonderful kiddie playground where a steep, snow-filled chute was the perfect place for sitting on their rumps and sliding like a couple of boys on bobsleds. Over and over they climbed back to do it again until one of the descending youngsters scooted full tilt into the other. Squalling with rage, they tore into one another tooth and claw, and mother had to lambaste them with her heavy paws to start them once more on the long journey to the green strip of meadow at tidewater.

In the bottomlands they would meet others of their own kind. Their unquenchable curiosity, their absolute gift for mischief, would involve them in endless scrapes from which they would have to be rescued by their mother. And she herself would become a parent of unpredictable moods. At times she would hold the fluffy little balls of fur close in her arms, crooning and loving them tenderly. Suddenly, for no discernible reason, she would cuff them until they bawled like spanked babies. In still another mood, she would turn over heavy boulders on the tide flats to expose crabs and little fishes hiding beneath. With the seafood course finished, she would lay heavy paws on meadow mouse runways to expose more tidbits. Always, she would defend the cubs with her life against all other living creatures, including other bears and man.

Gradually, through the summer months, the fierce female would wean her infants and teach them to earn their own living. She would show them which of the freshly sprouted grasses and shrubs were the tastiest; how to catch spawned-out salmon in the creeks; how to card wild berries from the bushes with their claws. And when the short Alaska summer drew to a close, when equinoctial gales off the Arctic ice pack drove them all to shelter, the she-bear would lead her cubs back into the wild tors and take them to den with her for another six months of winter. But with the coming of their second spring, the young grizzlies would be due for a surprise.

Once, on a day in early June, Andy Simons reported seeing a female and her two yearlings—teen-agers by human standards—come to a parting of the ways. Andy watched them let go, not willingly, from the mother's apron strings. The young grizzlies were now grown into husky 200-pounders, though still inclined to tag along behind the she-bear and even go to den with her that coming fall if she'd let them. But the youngsters Andy watched were not going to be so pampered. They were going to be deserted at the crossroads while their mother turned her back on them and took the high road to another romance.

Steered by a big, black-rubber nose which he kept extending and wrinkling, a huge brown boar came over a hilltop and plodded in a beeline toward the mother. At this ominous sight the yearlings called on mother to fight by squalling an S O S, but for once she paid no attention to their alarms. It was her second spring after giving birth to the cubs. She was no longer lactating, and her generative organs were prepared to start another family. She suffered the giant stranger to smell her all over, and she in turn nipped him encouragingly on the neck and seemed pleased when he fell in behind her, dogging her every step, nudging her persistently. The only time shaggy Romeo left the she-bear's flanks was to rush in open-mouthed irritation at the yearlings. Observed Andy wryly, it wasn't long before the lovers went one way and the castoff young ones another.

Through more than fifty years in bear country, Andy Simons came to know the ways of young grizzlies on their own, and declared that in this stage of life they are a puzzling mixture of caution and daring, bluff and curiosity. All bears are hard to figure out, Andy would say, but the young ones do the craziest things for which he had no words of explanation. Once he saw a 30-pound wolverine accost a grizzly ten times its own size on a narrow trail; the wolverine screeched and the young bear turned away. He saw one chomp down a hornet's nest with evident relish. Once a yearling followed his tracks all day. The next one he saw fled in terror. There's no logic behind their actions; they are in the learning period of their lives, wandering into strange places for no apparent reason. Often in their yearling summers, the grizzlies will scale dizzy peaks where even a mountain goat might give pause. And in this part of their young life, the yearlings will develop the art of rump-skiing to a hair-raising spectacle.

Among the glaciated mountains of Southeastern Alaska I once witnessed a death-defying descent. High up in the head of a snow-packed ravine I spotted a bear doing a balancing act along a wall of ice. Suddenly, it jumped off onto the almost perpendicular slope and came zooming out on the slick, wet ice of the glacier at a dizzy rate of speed. Then, to my complete amazement, it came sailing over the lip of the glacier to plunge fifty feet into a lake. Apparently, none the worse for its lofty belly-buster, the young grizzly paddled ashore and started climbing the slope again—just possibly to try it all over again.

On another occasion the crew of a government patrol vessel and I watched two yearling brown bears cavorting on a gale-swept beach of Unimak Island, far out beyond the tip of the Alaska Peninsula and the westernmost range of the grizzly bear in America. The turbid gray waters of Bering Sea were crashing in great frothing combers to hiss across the sands, and the young brownies were romping at the very edge, dashing in and out, snatching bits of kelp and flotsam and tossing them to one another in an exuberant game of catch. Time after time they dodged from under with not a second to spare before a curling wave thundered down on the spot where they'd been. They came a cropper finally when they seized and tugged at a bulky object and were buried under an enormous foaming breaker. For awhile we couldn't see them. Then they emerged like drowned rats, fought the undertow, and dragged what appeared to be the bloated carcass of a sea lion high and dry. They weren't playing any more. They were bickering over enough spoils of the sea to fill a dozen bears.

On the same ocean voyage, as we cruised offshore beyond a river mouth, we saw a half dozen or more young bears paddling up and down the swirling surf, and we knew with no further investigation that the migration of salmon into that stream had not yet started; that the brownies, like eager youngsters, just couldn't wait for the fish to move into the fresh-water shallows. They had to come out in the ocean to meet them. When one of the youngsters managed to pluck a salmon out of the waves he was pursued down the length of the beach like a football player headed for the goal posts.

An old-time gold prospector living a hermit-like existence

among the bears on Yakataga Beach in southern Alaska while
he operated a "surf-washer," invited me into his log cabin for
a cup of coffee and gossip. He told me that the most exciting
moments of his life had been spent "in company with a yearling brown bear." He went on to explain he'd been following
a bear trail along a glacial creek several years before, looking
for a place to ford the milky torrent. Suddenly, he'd heard a
loud snort in the bushes, and not being too choosy about where
he landed, he jumped into the creek and started for the other
side.

"Couldn't have picked a worse place," he groaned. "Stepped
right into a bed of quicksand."

Throwing himself full length across the crumbling wet sand,
the old surf-miner managed to claw his way to slightly firmer
bottom and was about to struggle to his feet when he looked
up. There, no more than forty feet away, was the bear
crouched on its belly watching him.

"I yelled at it to git away from there," continued the gold
rush pioneer. "It paid me no mind; just laid there givin' me
the eye like it was waitin' to see what *I'd* do about the
situation."

The slung rifle over his shoulder had not only been dunked
in the quicksand, but was jammed under his body where he
couldn't get it loose. "Mister," he said, "I figured I was in a
hell of a fix. I'd never wanted to kill a bear; never had to before, and this didn't seem to be the time to start tryin'."

Rubbing his gray stubble as he recalled the exciting moments, the old-timer poured us both another cup of coffee
before resuming. "I figured that if I came out of this mess in
one piece, it wouldn't be because of what I did, but what the
bear didn't do."

What gave the surf-miner some hope was his observation
that the bear was rather small as Yakataga brownies go. "I
figured it for a yearling," he told me. "It kept cockin' its ears
and sniffin' and tiltin' its head sideways at me, like it was more

curious than anythin' else; like it had never seen a man before at such close range and might never get a better chance.''

He wasn't out of the quicksand, either, reminded the old-timer. The stuff kept settling and he had to keep inching toward the bank, all the while talking to the bear until he reached the hard shoreline with no more than thirty feet now separating them. He said he worked his rifle free and wiped some of the silt off it, then took a chance and stood up. ''That's when the young brownie gives a *woof!* and goes traipsin' off into the brush.''

The hospitable sourdough walked me down to the beach to see me on my way. I watched him shovel the hopper of his homemade gold washer full and skid it out where the pounding surf washed the ruby sands clear, leaving specks of flour gold to form an amalgam with the quicksilver-coated riffles. He had one more message for me and he gave it to me when we shook hands goodby.

''Don't never send no hunters up here,'' he warned. If any showed up, he said, he'd be obliged to tell them there weren't any bears around, and this would make him a liar because ''the biggest dam' brownie in Alaska'' had been living for twenty years on a glacier creek close by.

''He's a whopper, and he minds his own business,'' said the old-miner. ''I've knowed him since he was a yearlin'.''

q The Canine Enemy

One summer I called on a stream watchman in Southeastern Alaska whose working partner was an irascible wire-haired terrier. "I keep him mean as poison on purpose," the stream guard told me. "My job is to tally the upriver run of spawner salmon. Little Pete, here, takes care of the bears."

We sloshed upcurrent in our rubber boots to a weir across the river and walked an overhead plank to an opening in the center where the salmon could be easily seen as they swam over a white-painted board. The watchman said there was only one trouble with the arrangement. The weir caused a pileup of fish below the narrow gate and the salmon concentration in turn attracted hungry grizzlies. This is where savage Little Pete earned his keep.

For awhile the moody mutt seemed to be eying the seat of my pants with growing irritation, and I was almost relieved to see a grizzly appear on the river bank below us. Instantly, Little Pete fairly detonated with rage as he blasted off the

plank runway and charged down on the 500-pound beast. I
can't really say I was surprised when the bear turned away
and started back into the woods with the terrier stinging its
rump like a gadfly, dodging swipes that would have belted him
halfway across the river if they had landed. Unperturbed, the
stream watchman worked the pushbutton counters in his
hands as he tallied salmon.

"Happens two, three times every day," he said laconically.

Since that summer I have many times seen big bears yield
to angry little dogs, and as often I have wondered why they do
it. Is it because the bear associates dogs with humans? Or is
the whole thing deeper rooted in time, perhaps millions of
years before man had even appeared on the planet, back when
the earth played host to those strange creatures which were
neither dogs nor bears, but something of both. Eventually and
ever so slowly, these dog-bears (or bear-dogs) forked apart,
each on its separate branch of the family tree. The bear
evolved into a morose giant who, except for mating and
mothering, preferred to travel alone. On the other hand, the
wild dog, including its close relative the wolf, adopted a gre-
garious form of existence. It learned to run in packs and it
learned a war cry.

To this day the bark of a dog, the howl of a wolf, seems to
stir a primordial warning device in the bear, harking back to
the dim eras when enormous bands of canines swept like
pestilence over the land. Their bark—or howl—was the rally-
ing call for others of their ilk to join in the blood purge, and
it spelled terror for those being pursued. This meant not only
the quondam beasts long gone from this earth, but contemporary species like moose and buffaloes, wild boars and the great
cats of the world, and bears. Early man rallied the dogs to help
him run down game. Here in America we used them on mountain lions, jaguars, and grizzly bears. As the big yellow bears
dwindled in the United States, dog owners turned to Mexico
for more of the same savage excitement.

In the 1930's several outfitters from the States were licensed to take their clients and strings of dogs down across the Mexican border for cougars, jaguars, and bears. There, as elsewhere, the baying of hounds never failed to rout the fierce yellow bear and send it loping into the sun-baked crags where it hoped no horse nor man might follow. Though the small Mexican grizzly, *oso grande*, still exists in the Cerro Campana some distance north of Chihuahua City, its range is probably less than 4 percent of what it was a hundred years ago, and a factor in its impending extinction was its ancient enemy, the dog.

A Mexican friend once put it this way: "When a bear hears one dog, it fears many."

Is there a close connection between this and the grizzly's relationship with wild wolves? An inkling of how it might have fared with them eons past comes out of an experience related to me by Frank Glaser, a government hunter stationed in Alaska a few years ago.

On a June morning Glaser lay hidden at a vantage point in McKinley Park, binoculars trained on a sidehill where a bitch wolf had dug her den and recently whelped. In the den the small pups were sleeping, and sprawled in the near vicinity as a sort of honor guard were the female's three young of the previous year. Though the yearlings were all larger than the parent female and fully able to forage for themselves, the family ties were strong between them. They all hunted and killed and fed together.

As is the habit of timber wolves at denning time, they had buried several game carcasses nearby, and the scent of the decaying meat had attracted a grizzly mother with three yearling cubs. Glaser's binoculars filled with bears as they drew near, swaggering along as though they owned the mountains. His first intimation of pending trouble came when one of the yearling grizzlies, itself a beast of 300 pounds, sniffed its way to within thirty feet of the den mouth. At this point every wolf

had secreted itself and was crouching—as Glaser put it—
"like coiled springs."

Frank thinks that the slant-eyed lobos had observed the
coming of the bears for considerable distance and had developed a plan. It was triggered into action when the unsuspecting yearling grizzly seized the carcass of a caribou and started
dragging it down the hill. There was a flash of leaping wolves,
and then they were swarming all over the young bear. The
small gray female kept snapping at its nose while the rest of
the pack tore at its unprotected hindquarters. When the
grizzly mother came roaring to the defense of her year-old cub,
all four wolves turned on her and she became the central
figure in a swirling mass before she realized what had happened. The wolves appeared to be just too speedy and elusive
for any of the bear's paw strokes to connect. This was their
kind of fighting; to rip and slash and leap away, and they went
at it like a gang of commandos. When the four bears managed
to maul their way clear of the hornets' nest into which they
had blundered, they scrambled full tilt for a nearby knoll.

The fight might have ended here if one of the yearling bears
hadn't found another cache of buried meat and stubbornly
set about digging it up. In the meanwhile, Glaser had discovered another wolf with his binoculars, a large coal-black male
weighing well over a hundred pounds, he thought. It came
running down a spur, touched noses briefly with the small gray
female, and immediately launched itself in an attack against
all four bears. It was met head on by the she-bear and they
engaged in a furious fang to fang encounter from which it
didn't seem possible the black wolf could emerge alive. The
bear cubs acted as if they couldn't make up their minds what
to do; but not for long, because suddenly all the other wolves
stormed up the knoll after them and a battle royal ensued.

As quickly as they had started it, the wolves shifted tactics.
All at once the entire band swarmed all over the smallest
yearling. They had suddenly become aware of its weakening

condition, and they sensed a kill. But at this moment, said Glaser, the grizzly mother made her own move. Roaring hideously and laying about her with swinging paws and snapping teeth, she drove her three young ones down into a patch of thick brush and through it to the bank of a glacial stream. The small yearling, now dripping blood and limping badly, continued out into the icy water and lay down up to its neck. Mother and the remaining two cubs backed into the river until it was too deep for the wolves to stand on their feet, then pivoted around to present a solid front of fangs and claws to the oncoming pack. Suddenly, as dramatically as it had begun, the grizzly-wolf fight was over.

Frank Glaser is too experienced in woodcraft and nature to infer from this one example that the wolf is equal to the grizzly in combat. Several other times in his Alaska adventures he has seen the lobo move casually out of the way when a big yellow bear came its way on a collision course. The government hunter thinks it took the stimulus of what amounted to an invasion of its home to rouse the wolves to do-or-die attack; the instinct, shared by nearly all animals, to protect its new born young against any odds. Nowadays, he reasons, when the earth is no longer ravaged by canine carnivores, there is considerable tolerance between the higher forms of predators. Each appears to have achieved its place, and aside from the necessity of gathering the kind of food it needs to survive, the flesh-eaters get along as well together as do most humans.

9 The Jinx of Sandy Lake

Andy Simons, who in his day led more hunters and camera buffs among the giant brown grizzlies of western Alaska than any other guide, once told me that the biggest bear he ever saw in fifty years was neither shot nor photographed. "That bear wass a jinx," declared Andy in a soft, slightly Finnish-accented voice.

His remarks came at the end of a long day as we rested in camp under an Autumn moon. He had crammed his big curve-stem briar with plug-whittlings, and the firelight was playing across his ruddy face and its week-old stubble as he puffed the tent full of fragrant tobacco smoke. We had dined like potentates on fried berry-fed ptarmigan and Andy was in a story-telling mood. "Let me tell you about that hoodoo brownie," began Andy. "It started with a wrecked airplane."

The single-engine plane was floating upside down in Sandy Lake, continued Andy, a junk-pile of twisted struts and water-logged fabric. But as the old guide's story opens, the bush pilot was making good time without it. He came banking around an alder patch at top RPM, yelling like a fire siren, zoomed across an open patch of muskeg to the lake shore and made a three-point landing in the rubber boat Andy was holding ready for him. At his impact, the boat shot clear and the guide began flailing the shallow water with the stubby, folding oars. There wasn't any time for talking, Andy told me; they already had their orders from two bears smashing through the alders.

One of the bears was a mustard-colored female of moderate size, weighing no more than 600 or 700 pounds. Her ears were flattened back ready for a brawl, and every hair on her back stood stiff as a porcupine quill. But mean as she looked, said Andy, she was baby stuff alongside the chocolate-hued monster at her shoulder. The sheer bulk of this second bear was enough to make even an old-time bear guide like Andy gasp for breath. Behind a head the size of an overstuffed Morris chair rose enormous humped shoulders and a great barrel of a body the size of a fat ox. One quick look told Simons that in all his years of guiding on Alaska Peninsula and Kodiak Island, he had never before run into the likes of this shaggy titan. This was, by far, the biggest of them all!

Still sprawled across the inflated sides of the rubber raft, his back toward the bears, the bush pilot faced downwind and tried to call out a course through bars and snags. Suddenly, he bellowed a hoarse warning but there was nothing Andy could do about it. A surging channel at the lake outlet had gripped the rubber bubble, spun it around, and started scooting it directly for the bank in front of the bears. Andy's short oars churned water to no avail. There was no fighting the current as it whisked the raft into an eddy under the very noses of the angry bears. "Ve vere sitting ducks," said Andy.

He looked up into the eyes of the great brutes as they stood together, staring down at the men with bold curiosity. The bush pilot started to twist around to see why Andy wasn't paddling any more, and at this the giant male lifted its black snout, extended its nostrils in an unmistakable gesture of belligerence and rose on its clawed toes until all four legs were stiff as ramrods.

The guide said he felt something being shoved into his hands. The bush pilot had been untying his rifle. Without taking his eyes off the bears almost straight overhead on the river bank, Andy threw a cartridge into the chamber and laid the gold bead on the point of a massive shoulder. But he didn't fire. I couldn't, he told me. This was no time to be shooting a bear, world record though he knew it had to be; he couldn't pull the trigger. Unless the beasts came bawling down upon them in a determined charge Andy made up his mind not to start throwing lead. They had troubles enough without starting any more.

It was a crazy situation they had gotten themselves into, explained Andy as he thumped the dottle out of his big curve-stem briar and recharged it again. The only way to make much sense out of it was to go back a couple of days, back to the night they had spent under a wildly flapping tent at the edge of the alders on Sandy Lake with their two hunters and the camp cook. Red-eyed, shivering, soaked to the skin, they had huddled around a smoking sheet-iron camp stove crammed with green alder wood. To understand their miserable condition, said the guide, I would have to know what it was like to be hunched under the sagging, rain-hammered canvas. I would have to feel the rain-gusts as the tent walls billowed and buckled. I would have to hear the thud of the gale against the anchored airplane out front. Before I could understand why Andy had no stomach for further trouble, I'd have to know what it was like to be camped directly in the path of disaster on that black night of hell when the williwaws came.

It had been raining heavily all that day and there had been no hunting. In the afternoon the wind started blowing from the mountain passes at the head of Sandy Lake, the fury of it mounting until the plane began yawing wildly at its anchor ropes. They were 600 miles west of Anchorage in one of the least traveled regions of treeless Alaska Peninsula. They needed that plane; there was no other way to get the hunting party back to civilization. Just before dark the bush pilot and Andy fought their way to a foam-heaped shoreline to double the mooring lines.

Wind velocity also doubled when the sun went down. There was no sleep for anybody when every blast threatened to strip the canvas off their heads. As the roof sagged under its load of water, tent stakes started pulling free of the mucky tundra. A dozen times one or another of the party crawled outside in the pelting rain to drive the pegs back and make fresh ties with the guy lines. By morning the wind was at hurricane strength. But still it blew, harder and harder, mounting to the violent climax that occurred at ten o'clock in the forenoon.

The camp stove had long since smoked out. The Simons party were all hunkered down on their sleeping bags, cold and soaked, nerves strung taut, when the members heard a new and ominous sound from up the valley. It was like a hundred express trains roaring down upon them, and they knew the moment they had all been dreading was at hand. The Aleutian williwaws, unpredictable twisters attaining speeds upwards of 150 miles an hour, were howling in for the kill. Andy says there wasn't time to think about it before a ripping windblast flattened the tent. For a moment nobody could breathe in the sudden vacuum. Then as they dug clear of the pressing wet canvas, they saw the plane! It was like a crushed bit of paper in the debris-laden sky; spinning, sailing, turning over and finally crashing on its back among the seething whitecaps. The pontoon landing gear, visible above the wave tops, raced crazily down the lake.

There wasn't much sense to it, Andy will admit, but he and the bush pilot started along the lake shore in pursuit. They didn't get anywhere. As soon as they moved out from the screen of alders they were bowled over by the screeching gale and were lucky to claw their way back to the anchored canvas. Said Andy ruefully, in an hour it was dead calm—only a 40-mile wind. While the rest of the party put the camp back in shape and combed the tundra downwind for blown equipment, Andy and the pilot went plane hunting. They found what was left of it off a rocky point in four feet of water. It would never fly again.

Then came the first small break in their string of bad luck. Andy remembered a small rubber life raft had been taken out of the plane for crossing rivers on bear scouting trips. Diligent search turned it up, after which they held a powwow in camp on how it might be used to best advantage. The two hunters and the cook would stay with the camp; Andy and the bush pilot would attempt to float down to Bering Sea and make their way along the coast to a salmon cannery at Port Moller where a wireless station could send an S O S to Anchorage. It was on their way down to Port Moller that Andy and the pilot met the angry brown bears. Chilled to the bone by the rubber boat ride, they were taking turns running up and down the shore to restore circulation when the bush pilot came running back with the cranky female and the chocolate-colored monster at his heels. Shortly afterward came the perverse current that swung the unwieldy raft ashore right under the waiting brown bears.

It was, as Andy put it, a crazy situation. The rarest bear trophy on the entire peninsula was standing on the bank over his head. One shot would have put his name at the head of the list of world-record holders. But even in so tense a predicament, Andy thought the matter through. The bears, though greatly agitated, had not charged them—not yet, anyway. They were still making up their minds. Besides, Andy figured the prestige of shooting such a trophy belonged not to the guide, but to his hunter. His job clearly was to reach a wireless station, try to bring out his hunting party intact, and not to do any shooting except in the direst emergency.

Like practically every decision I knew Andy to make in his five decades of guiding, this one worked out all right, too. When he and the bush pilot finally thrashed back into the current again and went bobbing down the river rapids, the two brown bears loped along the bank abreast of them, fading back only when the channel swung to the opposite bank and shortly flowed out into a salt-water bay. Without further mishap Andy and the pilot landed on a wild beach, deflated their raft and carrying it on their backs to cross other rivers, tramped the long weary miles to the wireless station. Some time later a relief plane flew the ill-fated hunting party back to civilization.

Simons went back another year, of course. The memory of the huge bear smash-banging through the alders behind the fleeing bush pilot, the way it looked on the bank above him like a hairy mammoth out of the Ice Age was too much for the guide to resist. When one of his favorite hunter clients wired him he wanted a record breaker, or no bear at all, Andy chartered another float plane for the flight to Sandy Lake.

He told me he had a good idea where the big fellow might be hanging out, and when he slipped away from camp alone to scout the tundra, he found its enormous pad prints punched deep in the silt along the river bank. No mistake, this had to be the same giant brownie. Said Andy, "I wanted to surprise my hunter, so I didn't tell him he was in for the most exciting bear hunt of his life."

The way it turned out, Andy is glad he didn't, because the jinx of Sandy Lake struck again. This time, a supposedly extinct volcano suddenly came to life and exploded over their heads like an H-bomb.

Old Veniaminof had been dormant for so many years that an ice-plug had formed over its crater and built to a dagger point in the sky. Its white slopes, rising to a glistening pinnacle, had long been a landmark for passing ships enroute between America and the Orient. On its high snowfields the big brown bears could be seen almost daily. Its cold, white majesty appeared to be the last place in the world for hell to come blasting to the surface.

The very next morning in camp Andy and the hunter came out of their tents on Sandy Lake to see a column of black smoke jetting from the summit of Veniaminof, ascending thousands of feet and becoming a fountain of color in the zenith. Rumbling explosions deep within the volcano hurled ashes and fire streaks, and soon the heavens turned from blue to sooty gray. The fumes of burnt sulphur stung their noses, but more insidious was the slow, steady settling of fluffy volcanic ash over the entire countryside. The clean, white snow on the mountains became black. The bears they had spotted through the binoculars became invisible, and now they could see only their trails.

With the fallout of cinders and ash, the bears began a massed migration from the slopes and across the tundra to feeding areas free of grit. High on the blackened mountainsides Andy and his hunter watched a spectacular show. The bears were throwing themselves forward in belly-buster slides, and they followed the bears' progress by the white streaks they left behind. Other brownies trudging stolidly down the mountain drifts left a slow accumulation of white dots on the black ash coating. It was a rare sight, said Andy, but it raised merry hob with their bear hunting.

Fortunately, the wind carried most of the black fluff and lava rock out over Bering Sea. This small security could change with a shifting of air currents to bury their campsite and taint every drop of water for miles around. Under the circumstances Andy decided it was no time to be looking for the world record brownie; to have done so would have been like looking for a needle in a burning haystack. The volcano was acting up worse than ever. Black, oily clouds rolled over the lip of its crater to spread a stifling blanket of smoke over the tundra. The sun went down in the center of the sky, and the ash deposit became inches deep. Their only drinking water now came from cans Andy had filled with lake water at the first sign of the holocaust. Danger mounted with every hour, and this time the guide knew he could not leave the camp to look for help. He had to stay with his hunter, come what may. Their only chance was that news of Veniaminof's rampage might have filtered into Anchorage and alerted the plane charter service to their predicament.

The hunter heard it first. Above the roar and crackle and deep explosions from the bowels of the crater, he heard the steady drone of a single-engine plane becoming steadily louder until it appeared through the reeking overcast, skimmed pontoons on Sandy Lake and came humming in on the step to their shore camp. There was no time for proper dismantling of camp and packing of equipment. Conditions were worsening by the minute. Stopping only long enough to gulp down a mug of hot coffee, the bush pilot hustled the stranded hunters into the light plane and took off from the water full throttle. Aloft, they could understand why he was in such a rush. Old Veniaminof was really blowing its top. The pilot said that homesteaders a hundred miles away had watched the sky turn black and sent in reports by their ham radios. For mile after mile the pilot flew blind through ebony clouds that tossed the little plane about like a cork on the ocean, and filled the cabin with choking fumes of brimstone. When they finally broke into the clear, it seemed to Andy as if he had never seen so bright a sun, or smelled sweeter air.

The hour was late when Andy Simons finished his story about the hoodoo brownie of Sandy Lake. The campfire in front of our tent had burned itself down to a bed of winking coals, and the guide's curve-stem briar was like another ember glowing in the dark. After awhile Andy spoke again: "I believe he is still there."

Unless old age has claimed him as he slept in his winter den high in the shadows of cantankerous Veniaminof, the monarch of all brown bears still lives; still comes shuffling down to the river for his salmon at spawning time. Somewhere in that bleak, lonesome land, guarded by fierce williwaw winds and the fires of infernal regions, the jinx of Sandy Lake may still be shaking the tundra with its mighty tread. The beast Andy Simons called "the biggest bear I ever saw" may still be leading its charmed life.

q A Guide Looks at Bears

Though Alaskans recognize Andy Simons as their number one all time guide, it is not so well known a fact that he rendered fully as valuable service as a member of the old Alaska Game Commission. Some of the measures he advocated at the early annual meetings, where I sat in as director, are practically enshrined in the regulations. It was Andy who quietly persisted from the beginning that the surest way to build up a depleted game species was to list it among the *shootable* where the sportsman's money and the warden force could be used to watch over it. In applicable terms this could mean establishment of sanctuaries where needed. It could mean shorter seasons, smaller bag limits, or perhaps no hunting at all until there was a surplus of breeding stock. Most of all, it meant active management.

This all tied in with Andy's years of observation—and this is very important—*that a certain amount of hunting by humans and pursuit by natural enemies sharpened the senses of wild game; that culling out the cripples and misfits was essential to healthy existence of the others.* He believed in hunting because it had been a part of his boyhood in Finland, and of man's survival since the beginning of time. He had studied enough game herds to know them for a renewable resource of the wilderness, which if not utilized would be sluiced down the drain of old age and disease. In Andy's book the wise use of wild game was to supply meat for the Indians and homesteaders. It was also the taking of trophies, usually old males nearing the end of their life spans, taken only after careful binocular study and parley between the guide and his non-resident hunter. And with Andy, every pound of usable meat must be salvaged.

Any number of visitors will attest Andy Simons' reluctance to let them squeeze triggers unless they were sure, very sure, that this was the trophy they wanted to take home from their Alaska adventure. We in the game commission chambers will remember Andy as the quiet man from the Kenai who prefaced every vote on a proposed new regulation with the gently probing question: "Is it right for the game?"

He never wavered from his opinion, strengthened every season he spent in the Alaska game fields, that properly regulated hunting offered no danger to the overall bear populations, but tended to stabilize their numbers. The greatest peril faced by the big bears, he thought, was not from sportsmen but from those who had no interest at all in their survival. Andy used to say that the real enemies of the grizzlies were people like the small group of cattle owners who demanded the extermination of the world famous Kodiak brown bear; like the commercial fish canners who begrudged the salmon eaten by bears along the coastal rivers; like the loggers working under permits issued by the United States Forest Service to strip the wooded islands of Southeastern Alaska, destroying the ancestral homes of the bears, leaving ugly desolation and rivers running with muck where salmon once spawned.

Andy Simons admired the great brown bears for their bold attitude toward man, and for their indomitable courage in facing up to rifle fire. He was no sentimentalist, however. He looked at bears with a hard eye when he had to, and didn't try to cover up for their faults. Sure, the brownie eats salmon, he'd say; he eats tons of them and sometimes he doesn't wait for them to spawn before catching them off the river riffles. And then he might add meaningfully that the brownie had been eating salmon for thousands of years, but still the rivers were full when the white man moved in with his nets.

Sure, the Kodiak brownie will eat cow flesh. But when Andy voted for a field man to spend several months on Kodiak Island checking up on "kills," it was found that almost all the cows had perished from malnutrition, overexposure, or falling off cliffs during the severe island winter before the brownie came along to scavenge the remains.

Sure, the grizzlies will charge a human once in a while. No one could ever pick an argument with Andy Simons on this, because he himself had been on the receiving end of several attacks. The surest way to bring one on, he declared, was to wound the bear, blunder into its meat cache, or tangle with a she-bear's cubs. Otherwise, it was Andy's experience that most grizzlies and big brownies would honor man with a dignified retreat. But don't crowd them! Give the big fellows a chance to look you over; give them time to study you and make up their minds. Then, maybe they'd go on about their business. Or then, again, maybe they wouldn't.

Remember this, Andy would say to a tenderfoot going on his first bear hunt, a brownie may look at you with complete recognition of what you are, yet make no move. It may hear you and still give no sign. But when it smells you it will make its move. It will get out of your way; it will stand its ground with clacking teeth and explosive snorts; or it will close in for a fight. In any case, son, you'd better be ready.

A lot of dangerous nonsense was being written and talked

about a brown bear being half blind, Andy would say. He had seen them spot the movement of a man a good mile away. Like most predatory animals the bear sees best directly ahead where it can bring both eyes to focus. Even then, Andy noted time after time, the mere sight of a man did not convey to the bear's brain the same kind of a jolt as that carried by the olfactory nerve. The nose governed, and that's why Andy always tested the wind when making a stalk, and kept taking looks downwind. No telling, he'd add wryly, when you might be the hunted instead of the hunter.

Unlike horned game which primes with the Autumn rut, bears are chiefly hunted in the springtime. The fur is still soft and glossy after the winter denning, and visibility is at its best because there are no leaves on the alders and willows. The high snowbanks on which the brownies like to travel and sleep at this season afford an opportunity to look them over with binoculars at distances of several miles, weeding out the small and medium sized bears and concentrating on the real big ones. Also, the long view prevents any possible mistake of shooting a female with cubs. Once, it permitted Andy and a hunter to witness a duel between two of the greatest carnivores still inhabiting the earth.

The arena was a snow-filled pass at the head of Lefthand Valley near the western tip of the Alaska Peninsula. A late May chinook breeze blew warm against the unshaven faces of the men that afternoon as they scanned the vast snowscape. Their eyes swept across the miles of undulating tundra, the foothills, and then the summit of Pavlof Volcano spouting ashes into the sky. Suddenly, they spied a pair of darkish objects so far away that Andy said they looked "like a couple of bugs on a crumpled bed sheet." The tiny figures drew closer together, rose upright and came together. Andy and his hunter reached for their binoculars in a hurry.

In the circle of the 7 x 50 glasses, magnified until they appeared to be within easy rifle-shot distance, two giant brown bears were locked in a fierce struggle. Toe to toe on hind feet, forelegs clinched around each other's necks, they slashed and raked with yellowed fangs. Breaking away for a moment, they spun around with ponderous agility and rushed headlong into another clinch; each bear trying to hurl the other down on the snow. There was no striking with the paws, even though they were big as smoked hams studded with baling hooks. The teeth were the main weapons, almost like a couple of half-ton dogs, each trying to crush the bones of his rival. Near the rim of Andy's binoculars a third bear showed. It was barely half the size of the furious gladiators, lighter colored and silkier furred. He knew it was the female in heat over which the battle was being fought.

"Bear down!" yelled the hunter.

When Andy's glasses swung back, the vanquished beast had struggled to its feet and was floundering off through the melting snow. The victor watched its beaten rival drag itself over a hill, then dropped to all fours and started plodding downhill toward the waiting female. Together, they vanished into a ravine.

Other brown bears were starting to show as far away as Andy and his hunter could see. The warm chinook wind that followed a freak 5-inch snowfall seemed to have started all the big bears swaggering down lover's lane together. Wherever they looked, Andy and the hunter spotted brownies in pairs and in groups up to four or five. It was the greatest massing of brown bears Andy had looked at in forty years. As evening came on to catch the two men struggling through the soft snow, they realized that night would be upon them long before they could win through to their beach camp at Cold Bay. Behind them, they saw bears in the dimming light. Between them and camp were others they would have to pass in the darkness. Both men knew that these bears, especially at mating time, would become much bolder after nightfall.

They were following the contours of a riverbed that would lead them to the beach, groping around a clump of alders, when a terrifying commotion broke out directly ahead. At least three bears, possibly more, had picked up their scent and were filling the night with deep-throated growls. These brownies were mad—really mad. Andy saw the alder tops sway violently against the barely visible skyline no more than forty feet away, and figured it for a bear slamming the brush to vent its rage. Immediately afterward there was a loud clacking of tusks by a second bear, and then a fearful bawl by still another.

Off to their side was a wide expanse of dead ryegrass beaten down by winter snows. Down its center ran a deeply padded trail, worn by the bears through years of travel. It was the main thoroughfare used by the giants of Lefthand Valley on their way from the high mountains to the coastal salmon streams, and it was certainly no place to walk in the dark if they wanted to avoid running into bears. But Andy said there wasn't any other choice. At least there would be enough light out there in the open to distinguish large objects. Backing slowly away from the bedlam in the alders, keyed to cut loose with their heavy rifles if they had to, they found a well-worn brownie trail and followed it toward Cold Bay. After a while they halted abruptly. In front of them loomed an object darker than the sky.

They waited, straining to see in the darkness. The obstruction didn't appear to move; perhaps it was a volcanic boulder, one of the hundreds spewed out by Pavlof in times past. There was but one way to find out. Guns at ready, they moved ahead until Andy's outstretched hand felt solid rock. Once past this imaginary hazard, they finished the night hike, and at two o'clock in the morning stumbled into their beach camp. A half moon, tattered with shreds of fog, was rising over the snow hills at the head of Lefthand Valley to cast its ghostly glow across the land. Andy felt the hunter's hand gripping his arm and looked around. One of the "rocks" they had just passed wasn't there any more.

Though Andy Simons looked at hundreds of Peninsula giant bears in his lifetime, he never claimed to understand their moody behavior. One of his favorite remarks was "if you know what a bear is going to do next, you know more than the bear does." I think I had better luck in guessing Andy's own moods. Any time I saw him fish his big curve-stem briar out of his mackinaw pocket and thumb it full of cut plug, I guessed he was in a mood for story-telling. One day as we sat by a trout stream, letting the weight of our packboards rest on the ground for a few moments, Andy said out of the blue sky, "I've seen 'em turn tail when they smelled me a mile away." He dragged at his pipe. "I've had one come close enough to slobber in my face."

It happened on the Bering Sea side of the Alaska Peninsula when the guide and a young photographer camped on the high cut bank of a river filled with spawning salmon. They'd rowed in from their anchored gas boat in a canvas boat, and used it for a tent by turning it over and propping up one side with the oars. Their sleeping bags were stretched underneath, and the open side was camouflaged with wild ryegrass. It wasn't much, but it was necessary if they wanted to be in their blind to start taking pictures at daylight next morning.

The night was black. Rain drummed steadily on the canvas bottom of the boat. In the total darkness they could hear the salmon thrashing in the shallows under the cut bank. Now and then there would be an outburst of grunts and splashes from the feeding bears. The big brutes were all around, and Simons said he didn't blame the young fellow for going to bed with his rifle. There was one old boar who kept sounding off with lusty roars. There wasn't a tree for two hundred miles, and he hoped the big brownie didn't come wandering up the bank and find them.

During the nerve-racking hours of the night, Andy's young companion sat upright every time he heard the swish, swish of a passing bear. And then in the graying dawn he fell into a troubled sleep. Andy guessed he must have dozed off, too, because the next sound he heard was a gurgling gasp at his side. The lad's face was white as chalk and he appeared to be in the throes of a nightmare. But it wasn't any nightmare; it was the real thing, because the boy was staring directly upward into the muzzle of the giant boar. The enormous beast must have arrived in complete silence. With catlike stealth it had eased its three-quarter-ton bulk through the tall ryegrass, thrust a barrel-sized head through the flimsy screen and now stood with rain dripping off its jowls within inches of the men.

There was nothing Andy could do except wait, and hope the young man didn't panic. The great bear was in control. If it chose to, it could kill them both, and it was undoubtedly quite aware of this. The boy didn't have the slightest chance of using his rifle, and Andy said he would always be glad he didn't try. Only by remaining quiet, letting the bear fill its nose with human scent and giving it a chance to withdraw with dignity—if it would—might they be able to squeak through one of the touchiest situations the guide had ever been in.

"That young fellow had guts," declared Andy. A taste of what the lad was enduring came the guide's way when the bear swung its broad muzzle to stare at him, and a shower of slobber and rain fell on his face. Andy never could guess how long this nose to nose encounter lasted between them. At the end, the bear turned for one more look at the young man, then withdrew its head through the ryegrass screen. They didn't hear a sound for several minutes, and realized the shaggy giant was standing silently outside waiting for one of them to make a move. After a long time, its padded feet thumped softly on the sopping ground as it slipped away. Said Andy, "I reached over and shook the hand of a brave young man."

He was braver than the guide thought. When the gray sky

lightened and cleared to give them a meter reading, they poked the camera lenses out through the curtain of wild rye-grass and together filmed a total of seventeen individual brown bears wading into the current to catch salmon. The boy waited in vain to see a brownie scoop a fish out with its paws, as his storybooks had pictured it, but it never happened. The brown-ie's method was to dunk its head into the water, seize the salmon in its teeth, and carry it ashore. Mostly, then, it crouched over the salmon and held it down with the front paws while ripping the red flesh free of the backbone. Glauc-ous gulls came screaming to peck at the remains, and a pair of bald eagles came flopping in at regular intervals to ferry the bear discards to their aerie atop a pinnacle rock.

Several times the giant boar, dominating the pool, reared to its haunches to study the overturned boat above him. As the day wore on its irritation mounted, and once it came rushing across the river and climbed part way up the steep bank to bawl its anger. All this Andy noted with concern, and during a lull in late afternoon fishing operations when the bears were back in the brush sleeping off their salmon jag, he slid the canvas boat down into the current and beckoned the photog-rapher to get in so they could head for the ocean. "Or do you want to spend another night here?" he asked.

The young cameraman was equal to the occasion. "No use to," he replied as Andy started pulling at the oars. "I'm all out of film."

q The Boy and the Bear

In his long career of guiding people in all age classes Andy Simons noted that while young hunters might be scared stiff at their first closeup look at a big brown bear, they had the resiliency to bounce back quickly. They were ready—even eager—to try it all over again. The same experience came my way quite by accident when I took my 14-year-old son out for what I thought was going to be a duck hunt.

The day was right for them. Williwaw winds howled as they pushed a storm front in from the Gulf of Alaska to wet down the primitive forests of Admiralty Island. Occasional dark thunderheads, veined with fire, flung barrages of sleet against our slickers. The violence was widespread over the subarctic, forcing the last migrating waterfowl of the season southward out of the Bering Sea tundra. Squinting our eyes against the stinging ice pellets, we could see smallish flocks sideslipping down to rest for a while on Admiralty Island's sheltered coves. It was a day for ducks, all right. It was also a day for trouble.

The first hint of that trouble came right after my valued old fishing partner Pete Peehan brought us to the wilderness island aboard his double-ender salmon troller *Helldiver* and helped my son and me slide a skiff into the salt chuck. We all rowed ashore and the bow of the dinghy grated across one of the enormous brown bear pad prints that were sunk deep into the beach rubble. They looked like the spoor of a prehistoric monster, but with a difference; the tracks were no more than an hour old.

Old Pete eyed the hat-size prints, then stooped to measure them with spanned fingers. "Not likely you'll be runnin' into that b'ar," he mused, "but if you do, you'll be looking at one of the biggest brownies on the island." He paused a moment before setting off down the beach with a No. 2 shovel to dig a bucket of butter clams for supper that night aboard the *Helldiver.* "Stand clear and don't rile him none."

Young Frank and I trudged the other way toward the freshwater inlet, following the platter-shaped indentations made by the bear. On the wide expanse of tideflats there was little risk of encounter with the big beast. There was even less chance when the tracks swung away from the beachline and disappeared into the gray-shrouded timber. It was well along in October. A wet chill filled the air, and new snow covered the peaks. It was high time the Admiralty Island brownies were plodding into the rugged high country to locate their winter dens.

"That's the last sign we'll see of that big bruiser," I promised my teen-age son.

Twenty minutes later I wasn't so sure. Where the creek formed a delta and spilled its numerous channels across the kelp-strewn flats we began splashing among salmon. Most of them were spawned-out carcasses of chums and humpies,

dead and dying like all Pacific salmon at the end of the first
spawning, and drifting downriver. But others flurried vigorously under our boots; late-run cohos plump with roe, fighting
their way up to the spawning riffles where they'd been hatched
three years earlier. I couldn't help recalling what a coastal
Indian once said: "When salmon in creek look out for bear."

We hadn't yet fired our guns. The stray mallards we put
up along the waterline flushed wild. We hunkered down behind
the nearest driftwood snag hoping they'd circle back, but none
did. All the puddle ducks that rose ahead of us flew straight
to the river mouth and settled down out of sight. The only
waterfowl left in the gusty turbulence of the bay were strong-
fleshed scoters, old squaws and gaily daubed harlequins. All
the other birds, including a big flock of soot-colored geese
known in Southeastern Alaska as "homesteaders," headed for
the creek.

Now we had them bottled up, I figured. When we moved
into the slot cut by the stream bed between towering evergreens and started shooting, the birds would come peeling
down the alley overhead faster than we could pull triggers and
reload. I'd been there before and worked the trick. I told
young Frank, "Now, you'll see something!"

The creek was dammed by a fallen spruce log at the edge
of the timber, forming a shallow pool lush with pond weeds.
The place had never failed to be crowded with feeding geese,
mallards, sprigs, widgeons, and fat little green-winged teal.
Sometimes there'd be so many upended ducks you couldn't
see the water for wiggling butts. The secret feeding spot was
bordered by waist-high beach rye, now turned straw color by
the cold nights. It formed a perfect screen for a stalk. I knew
just how to make the sneak, but one look at the eager face of
my teen-ager told me who expected to play Indian this time.

Leaning close so I'd be heard above the thudding williwaws,
I shouted, "No potshooting, young feller. Pick your bird on
the rise and stay with it."

The boy grinned—he'd been schooled in all this before—and slipped a "Roman candle" into his single-barreled .410. Then he was off on an adventure he would never forget.

The flight line of escaping ducks and geese from the creek would, I knew, be down the main creek to tidewater; so I picked a waterlogged stump and waited for young Frank to rouse out the birds. Though I was a good two hundred yards from the hidden pool, I kept my head down. The element of surprise was all on our side, or so I thought.

I watched the boy swing wide across the tidelands before skulking up to the edge of the standing rye surrounding the hidden pool. He stopped at the edge to fumble in his pockets. I couldn't help smiling because I knew what the boy was up to; he was placing a couple of extra .410 shells between the fingers of his left hand ready for quick reloading—another trick I had taught him. He looked my way in a cautious "all's well," then dropped to all fours and started creeping through the tall grass toward the shock of his young life.

When he was out of sight I upped periscope from behind the stump. All was quiet. Nothing had disturbed the birds, nothing at all; not even the sopping-wet brown bear that came padding silently out of the fog-hung timber and waded straight into the pool!

For a moment I couldn't believe my eyes. Then, with no awareness of how it happened, I found myself out in the open waving my sou'wester hat and hollering at the top of my voice. There was not the slightest response. The bear, with its huge head under water grabbing at salmon, the unsuspecting boy worming toward it through the ryegrass; neither saw me nor heard my shouts across the windswept flats. It was like a horrible dream.

As the distance between the boy and the bear narrowed to the showdown point, the agonizing thought came to me that these brownies were never more dangerous than just before denning time. Not even the most experienced guide with a big

.375 rifle wanted to face them at pointblank range—and I'd put a 14-year-old boy out there with a popgun.

I was running and yelling now, but with almost no hope of creating a diversion in time. My finger was on the trigger of my 12-gauge automatic, ready to fire a salvo of duck loads into the air. I couldn't do it. When young Frank heard the reports, the waterfowl would be flushing. They would almost surely cause him to rush out to the edge of the pool for a clear shot, and bring on a head-on meeting with the bear while I was still too far away for me to do anything about it; that is, if I could do anything at all.

Already, I was too late. The bear's hackles suddenly stood straight on end and its legs stiffened. It had picked up the hated human scent. It knew. I saw it rise out of the river with a salmon in its teeth, swaying like a humpbacked ogre out of another age. It snorted and dilated its nostrils to pinpoint the smell, then reared to full height, the water pouring off its paws. The rounded ears clamped back against the skull, the salmon dropped from its teeth, and a blood-chilling *whuff*! belched from its belly. It was at this instant that young Frank stood up in plain sight and looked into the hideous face of the bear.

I wasn't close enough to read the terror in his eyes as he recoiled from danger. Then boy and bear blurred in a wild confusion of a thousand pairs of thrashing wings erupting out of the pond and streaming my way—puddle ducks, home-steader geese, and a scrambled conglomeration of mergansers, gulls, ravens, squawking blue herons, and screaming bald eagles. Diversion? This was it.

By the time the last bird cleared the pond I had raced close enough to draw the bear's notice. It dropped to all fours and came my way stiff-legged through the shallows. Out of the corner of my eyes I saw a paralyzing sight. Young Frank had pulled down on the huge beast with his little .410.

"No! No!" I must have sounded like a steam calliope. The

smidgin of birdshot would only prick the excited giant into a rage. "Don't shoot," I yelled. "Start backing away slow!"

At the sound of my raised voice the bear gave me all its attention. With five heavy duck loads that I could put out in less than that many seconds, I'd already decided to let the monster come very close before cutting loose. But I didn't like the odds, and I followed young Frank's example by stepping backwards, fully expecting the bear to break into its charge at any instant. But it did no more than keep pace until it came to the lower end of the pond. There it hoisted both front paws to rest on the log to watch while the boy and I faded away from its private fish pond. Then it retraced its steps to the head of the pool, picked up the salmon it had dropped, and vanished under the big trees.

The boy joined me out on the tideflats. I thought he'd had enough excitement for one day, but he was all agog for more adventure. He pointed toward the bay where the waterfowl were circling in the storm clouds and wheeling back to the pond. "Let's hide behind a stump and take 'em on the way in," he pleaded. "Let's finish that duck hunt."

9 **The Exciting Forest**

A man is keyed up in the Alaska forests; he's wide awake, and he'd better be, because the grizzlies have made these woods the most exciting and dangerous in America. When a man leaves the highways or the beaches and plunges into the woods he can never be sure when he will run into a cantankerous bear who thinks it has a better right to these primitive forests than any human. On fishing trips at least one member of the party carries a rifle slung over his shoulder. Even then, action comes so fast he may not be able to use it.

On a July day I was showing a New England visitor one of Admiralty Island's wonderful fishing streams when grizzly trouble happened in a flash. Bill and I were following the contours of a timber-shadowed river back into the primitive woodlands. Bill had noted the excellence of the trail, how smoothly it had been worn, how well it curved about through the giant tree trunks, and he guessed that quite a few fishermen must be using it. I had to agree with him in all respects, but with one added bit of information. The fishermen were grizzly bears. Their "road" had started from the high mountain valleys and led down the streamside to tidewater, with spur lines running down to favorite fishing pools in the river. No human had traveled this trail for weeks.

A heavy rifle loaded with 220-grain slugs was cradled across my left arm ready for fast action, although I had no intention of using it unless a grizzly forced the issue. At this midday hour most of the bears should be well back in the dark timber napping soundly after a morning of salmon-gorging. They would not stir about again until late afternoon, though one couldn't be sure, as we soon learned. Where Bear Avenue led along the rim of a hemlock-shrouded canyon a hundred or so feet above the chattering river, I glanced down through an opening and froze in my tracks. With a forefinger across my lips I shushed Bill to silence, and pushed him down on a moss-covered hummock. Below us, within a pebble's toss, a brindle grizzly lay sprawled on her side, fondling her two small cubs.

Rising air currents were carrying our scent upward and away from her, and she was completely unaware of our hateful presence. It was an exciting situation. Luck was with us—for a few moments.

After an interval of tense watchfulness on our part, the she-grizzly rolled lightly to her feet and waded out into the current. The cubs followed until the swift water was too deep for their short legs, then lifted up on their haunches, whining with anticipation while mother plunged her jaws into the white water and lifted out a yard-long dog salmon. She bore it ashore almost directly below us, the cubs following eagerly. Holding the fish down with her forepaws, the female gripped it just below the gills with her front teeth and ripped the hide off one side to bare the pink flesh. The cubs shoved in to sink their baby teeth into the soft meat, squabbling and shouldering one another aside in fits of temper, their tantrums becoming so fierce that the mother sent them howling with spanks from her big paws.

The next development in this forest drama came with such suddenness that both Bill and I were taken by surprise. A perverse twister came downdrafting through the tree tops and must have carried our scent to the bears. The female let go with a throaty ejaculation and came bouncing to her feet stiff-legged as she tested the air currents with a thrust-out black nose, facing about rapidly in an attempt to locate an enemy she would attack the instant she had it spotted.

Suddenly, the worst possible thing happened. The cubs, squealing with terror, scuttled out of sight into the heavy underbrush of the canyon slope, headed straight toward our position on the rim. Their fat little brown shapes whizzed past us within ten feet, and I knew the raging she-bear would be right at their heels.

How she missed trampling over us, I'll never know. Her eyes, green with madness, were level with ours as she rushed by us to overtake her fleeing cubs. A few yards up the slope she caught the full force of our rising odors and let loose with a maniacal moan of anguish. Not until then did I have time to swing about with rifle ready for a desperate snap shot. Five minutes of charged silence went by before we heard her again. She was a quarter mile away, still urging her babies away from an enemy she dreaded above all living creatures, but whom she would fight to the death if need be.

I turned to Bill to congratulate him for keeping so cool. He seemed to be in a trance. "Great Gods," he declared. "I couldn't have lifted a finger if I'd wanted to."

My New England guest Bill was luckier than a well-known Juneau guide who left his rowboat to walk up one of these same Admiralty Island bear trails. Ralph Reischl was one of the most capable woodsmen and deadliest rifle shots in Southeastern Alaska. He was not only thoroughly experienced in the ways of grizzlies, but enjoyed walking alone in the forests for the thrill of seeing them. But something went wrong this time. No one will ever know what happened to him in the eerie, moss-shrouded timber. Search parties combed the forest for weeks without turning up a clue. They concluded that he had been ambushed by a grizzly and went to his death under its slashing fangs.

Another man who might have had a similar experience lived to tell about it. He was moose hunting near Mile 90 on the Glenn Highway when he came upon a grizzly in a small clearing, and though he succeeded in getting off a rifle shot, he was bashed to earth a split second later. Rolling himself into a ball to protect his vital under parts, the moose hunter was fearfully mangled and left for dead by the bear. He managed to drag himself to the roadside where a passing motorist rushed him to a hospital in Palmer. It took 250 stitches to close his gaping wounds. Later, they went back and picked up his rifle. It was bent like a boomerang.

The dean of Alaska guides, Andy Simons, and his partner Hank Lucas, often stated that the Kenai Peninsula forests harbored the most dangerous grizzlies in Alaska. They laid this to the bears' diet of moose calves, mountain marmots, and winter-killed carcasses of big-game animals. More unprovoked attacks on humans seemed to occur among these heavy flesh-eaters of the Kenai than anywhere else in Alaska. Of this, young Nick Lean, who lived at the outlet of Kenai Lake, will bear testimony for as long as he lives.

Young Nick and an older companion were scouting the Kenai Range for Dall mountain sheep when Nick walked under an overhanging ledge, heard a slight noise, and looked up just in time to glimpse a huge yellowish creature sailing toward him through the air. There wasn't time to shoot, so agile young Nick made the next best move, and it probably saved his life. He dove headfirst under a snow-flattened riot of alder brush just as the bear landed. The beast was pawing and raking furiously to get a good hold on Nick when his hunting partner rushed to his rescue. Though he shot the grizzly off the young man, the bear had lived long enough to rip deep gashes on his back and shoulders, and had come close to tearing his arm off.

Swathed in bandages, young Nick said generously that he didn't think the grizzly was after him at all. "It thought I was a mountain sheep."

If the big bears ever had cause to deliberately get a human it would be an early-day character known as Ivanovitch who made a business of hunting them for their hides. Ivanovitch received $10 a hide, crudely cured, delivered to the trading post. For this kind of money, even 70 or 80 years ago, Ivanovitch had to have quantity production. He had to work at his trade every day, taking his bears as he found them—cubs, yearlings, sows, and old boars. His killing weapon was the biggest "coal-burner" (black powder) rifle available in those early years, and it lobbed a thumb-sized slug at close range with deadly results. Ivanovitch stretched the freshly-skinned hides on sidehills, pegged flesh side up, and let sun, wind, and rain do the curing until he had a boatload ready to take into the trading post. None among the present generation seems to know what fate finally befell hide-hunter Ivanovitch. Many believe a bear got him.

There wasn't any doubt about what happened to the Indian over on Molina Bay who shot a brownie with one of the old .45-90 trade guns. The bear dragged its bleeding hulk into the alders and the Indian followed its blood-drenched trail. When he didn't get back to the family beraberi that night the natives put out a search party. They found their Indian brother curled near a small fire he had lived long enough to build. His chest and throat had been torn away and he had bled to death.

The throat-pulsing, hypnotic force that seizes upon a hunter to rob him of his coordination; the phenomenon that deer hunters call buck fever, is infinitely worse when the quarry is a grizzly bear that may kill you if you miss. Several years ago the contemporary world champion marksman visited the Alaska forests to take a trophy. His mission ended in failure, and he was man enough to tell me why.

"I'd been grouping my shots within an inch circle at a hundred yards," he let me know, "so what happened when a thousand pound bear showed up at the same distance?" He threw up his hands in despair. "I missed the beast completely. It was big as a load of hay, and I never touched a hair."

He offered no alibi, which was not the case with another visiting nimrod who claimed he could shave the whiskers off a mountain goat at a half mile. But that was before he saw his first grizzly high up in the wild forests of the Alaska Range. The hunting party of which he was the star had been traveling by packhorses toward Mount McKinley, which towered remote and beautiful more than 20,000 feet into the blue sky. In the thin, crystal-clear air the great white peak, 150 miles distant as the raven flies, appeared to the sharpshooting member to be no more than a couple of gunshots away. After a week of steady travel, it looked the same: a shimmery, snowy, unattainable mass of whiteness floating forever ahead.

About the time when the hunter had lost all sense of measuring distance, the guide said they ran into a fine, yellow grizzly standing on a nearby ridgetop silhouetted against the great mountain. Dismounting from his horse, the self-styled crackshot sprayed bullets all over the mountains until his gun was empty. At the end the bear still stood, aloof and motionless. It was then that the hunter came up with an alibi to end all alibis. Turning to the guide he said casually, "Guess I wasn't as close to that bear as I thought."

Like the stage of human life itself, the Alaska wilderness can be a scene of humor or tragedy, depending on what happens when a grizzly is encountered and on how well the man has learned to read the signs of grizzly behavior. At the outset, this much must be recognized: Though the bear's chances for survival depend on man's attitude—his mercy, really—the grizzly will do little to curry favor. The great beast will remain what it always has been down through the ages: moody, belligerent, unchanged, unbowed before man. Its sin is that it has not learned to be afraid of us, like other animals.

Let the shadow of a low-flying airplane fall across another big-game animal and it will race away in panic. But not the grizzly! It will, instead, rear up on its haunches and lay about it in fierce swipes. Bear "scaring" devices like pebbles rattled in buckets, fog horns, shrill whoops, hat waving, whistles, and gun shots may only further enrage a grizzly already angered. The man who turns tail and runs when meeting a grizzly invites disaster. The chances are that it will face you only long enough to make sure of your identity, then—if you give it a dignified chance—it will go on about its business. Rarely it will not, and then you must be prepared to give way yourself, or fight it out.

Today, the Alaska forests are exciting and to some extent dangerous, but they are changing fast. Only thirty years ago there were probably more bears than people in Alaska. But now there are four times as many humans up there, and undoubtedly fewer bears. If the population of Alaska continues to expand at its present rate—and it is likely to be further accelerated—the next generation or two may see the last stronghold of the grizzly overrun with settlers. The giant carnivores may either be gone from the country, or a remaining few may be driven into small pockets mostly behind wildlife refuge signs. Of all the big-game species with which the subarctic tundras and forests were endowed, its super-grizzlies are the front runners for extinction.

If there is any hope of preserving this sometimes dangerous, always exciting shaggy giant right out of the Ice Age, it must be done in the northwestern forests. There is no other place.

q The Unfair Chase

Of the seventeen other western states where the grizzlies once swaggered in numbers far greater than are presently in Alaska, thirteen of them have totally exterminated their big yellow bears. The small, scattering populations that remain are by comparison smallish beasts markedly inferior to the giants now treading southern Alaska's tundras and lurking in its primitive forests.

The question naturally arises, "How does the new state evaluate these great bears entrusted to its care?" Can it perpetuate them where other states failed? Is it of a mind to try?

In its final report to the Secretary of the Interior, the old Alaska Game Commission, which had been an instrument of the National Government and the Territory of Alaska from 1925 to 1959, said that the big bears were holding up well. The colorful, cantankerous carnivores were, in fact, contributing to the economy through attraction of nonresident hunters and photographers who left important money in the local treasury through fees for licenses and guides. The numbers of trophies being exported from the Territory was reported to be well within the rate of annual increase. With this statement, the old commission turned over controls to the new State of Alaska Department of Fish and Game.

How have the big bears fared since this takeover in 1960?

The state game keepers got off to a fine start by adding a requirement that all bear hides must be presented for sealing with serially numbered metal tags, thus setting up the means for computing annual kills, where and when taken, and other valuable data. Thus, in the year of 1961 the department was able to publish that 468 brown-grizzly bears had been shot; which, of course, could not account for the bears surreptitiously killed and not reported. Most of the recorded kills had been made in the areas where the largest specimens were known to live; Alaska Peninsula and the islands of Kodiak, Admiralty, Baranof, and Chichagof, also Kenai Peninsula and the coast of Prince William Sound. Only random kills were made, or at least reported, from the interior mountain ranges where the smaller grizzlies lived. Almost half of the bears had been taken during the spring months of April and May, not long after the animals came out of their winter dens.

The state game personnel also conducted aerial surveys directed toward faster and better ways of estimating bear populations. It adopted the more important refuge areas formerly established, and in some districts it lowered the annual bag limit from two to one. Only in the interior where it felt not enough hunters were being attracted to crop off the surplus did it recommend more liberal seasons for shooting. Then it bumped squarely into one of Alaska's most difficult and complicated problems: How to cope with the steadily growing business of hunting big game from small airplanes.

Its predecessor, the old Alaska Game Commission, had regulated against use of aircraft thusly: "No game animal shall be taken from or by means of an aircraft." A further

proviso said that, "no aircraft . . . shall be used for the purpose of driving, herding, or molesting the game animals,"
which included the bears.

The incoming Department of Fish and Game followed with
similar, but somewhat less restrictive measures. Under pro-
hibited methods its regulations provided, "by use of aircraft
. . . for the purpose of driving, herding or molesting game."
The use of helicopters in any manner, including transportation
of game, hunters, or hunting gear was expressly forbidden.
But somehow a loophole big enough to fly a small plane
through without scratching a wing tip was found, allowing
the business of flying guide service to boom in a big way.

The reasoning behind the reluctance to completely ban all
airborne big-game hunting in Alaska goes back to the early
days of bush flying in Alaska and Canada. The vast distances
of roadless wilderness between one community and another
brought about the development of air travel to an extent never
dreamed of by outsiders. Pioneers of the north stepped into
small airplanes equipped with either skis, pontoons, or wheels
with the easy assurance of a stateside resident driving his
family car, calling a taxi, or taking a bus. This meant flights
over the most primitive game fields on the continent, very
often at little more than treetop level. It meant the frequent
sighting of bears and other game. It led to the use of slow-
landing aircraft capable of alighting on sandbars, snowbanks, lakes, rivers, even glaciers and mountain tops near
spotted game. Very often a nervy pilot could put his passenger
right alongside the game. All the hunter had to do was step out,
shoot, and in a matter of minutes load the spoils aboard.
Alaska, once the most difficult terrain in America, quickly
succumbed to the little airplane.

No longer was it necessary for a nonresident sportsman to
make long-range plans for strings of packhorses, packers,
guides, and cooks. No longer must he live in tents pitched in
the mountain solitudes. No longer must he hike and climb, eat

camp chuck, and be forced to enjoy the scenic beauty. That was old stuff now. Just jump in a plane! Swoop down on the helpless beasts; pin them down where they couldn't get away! Zoom back to town the same afternoon!

So the new breed of flying guides started advertising "quickie" hunts, "instant" bears. In any number of instances the client from Bigtown was counseled by the pilot-guide to take it easy in the town cocktail bar. He'd fly out to scout the country for a bear and when he found a good one he'd be back to pick up the client. "I'll even lend you the gun," he'd say.

Deluxe service was provided by landing a hunter and guide while a pilot soared aloft to direct the "sportsman" to the bear floundering in the soft snow of spring. If the panicked beast tried to plow its way to the safety of brush, it could be literally herded toward the waiting guns. Illegal, but how could it be proved in court! The dead bear was all that counted.

On polar bears it was, and still is, licit procedure for two lightweight, ski-equipped planes to fly from Eskimo villages out over frozen international seas for many miles. When a big enough white bear is sighted, one of the planes—the one they call the "safety" plane—remains in the air to direct traffic while the other plane lands as close to the bear as the ice conditions will permit. The hunter, perhaps setting foot on Arctic ice for the first time in his life, steps out to gun down the helpless beast. Pausing only long enough to pose for the customary photograph with the downed bear, he flies back to the village. This procedure, incidentally, has now been condemned by many national sportsmen's organizations and penalties are invoked against it.

The pilot-guides see another side of the coin. Their "quickie" hunts are but a natural outgrowth, they say, of "everybody flies in Alaska." They point to the large sums of money they have invested in aircraft, and the personal perils involved in promoting faster service to visiting sportsmen. The same sort of efficiency is available to local residents flying out for a winter's supply of moose or caribou venison where no other means of transportation is feasible. Nor do they apologize for their kind of sports hunting.

"Why waste a month to shoot a bear?" some of them have been known to ask. "We can get you there in minutes. The old horse and packboard days are over. Alaska has speeded up and this goes for bear hunting, too."

What hasn't speeded up, however, is the very slow rate of reproduction and replacement of trophy-sized bears. It still takes a female two full years, often three, to produce a cub or two. Only half the cubs will be males. Only a few males are capable of developing to large size, and it will require several years for them to do it. As one of the game men told me not long ago: "They can't be turned out like hatchery trout." He summed up his observations. "Shortcuts to shooting off our big bears faster is certainly no help toward adequate protection. If there's one modernization we can get along without, it's for fliers to figure out speedier ways to knock off the giant bears."

There is, furthermore, the matter of fair play. Of this, the highly respected Boone and Crockett Club, which was founded in 1887 by Teddy Roosevelt, has taken full cognizance. As keeper of the records on big-game trophies, as well as being stanch advocates of sound conservation, the club has adopted these rulings: *Spotting or herding Land Game from the air or landing in its vicinity for pursuit shall be deemed Unfair Chase and unsportsmanlike. No trophy obtained by Unfair Chase may be entered in any Boone and Crockett Big Game Competition.*

Many rules of this world-famous organization have been converted into law by various states and countries. There is hope that the Alaska Department of Fish and Game may do the same with regard to airborne sports hunting. It will not be easily effected in a region so sparsely settled, so dependent on plane transportation for its normal means of travel. Alaska people are bound to go places, fish and hunt with fullest possible use of aircraft, and they will resent unwarranted interference.

Presently, only one out of the twenty-six Game Management Units into which the State of Alaska has separated its hunting regions conforms fully to the "fair chase" standards of the Boone and Crockett Club and the Alaska Big Game Trophy Club. It is Unit 9, embracing the Alaska Peninsula from Cook Inlet to the Aleutian Islands, home of the brown titan *Ursus gyas*, which shares top billing with the Kodiak bear, *U. middendorffi*, as the mightiest land carnivore extant. The special protection is conveyed in these words: "No person may use an aircraft in Game Management Unit 9 in any manner as an aid in taking big game except transportation to a pre-existing camp or to a site for the purpose of establishing a camp. When an aircraft is used for transportation within Game Management Unit 9 a camp must be established prior to hunting or taking game."

This restriction does not apply to Kodiak Island in Unit 8, nor to any other of the twenty-four units stretching from Southeastern Alaska to the Arctic Ocean. Although this means that under the Alaska law it is permissible in about 95 percent of the hunting area to fly within gunshot of a grizzly, then step out and shoot it, a trophy so taken will still not be eligible for recognition under the higher ethics required by the Boone and Crockett Club. At least one sportsman's group in Alaska has supported the Boone and Crockett ruling by requiring its members to sign a "fair chase" affidavit on bears and other big-game trophies submitted for competition. They do not condone as fair chase the spotting of big game from helicopters or fixed-wing aircraft, nor the subsequent landing in natural habitat and pursuit thereof. Says the Alaska Big Game Trophy Club, "Trophies taken in such manner are not eligible for recognition, for registration, or for award."

Urban C. Nelson, last executive officer of the old Alaska

Game Commission—a position held by the writer for several
earlier years—told me this: "I have heard many complaints
from *guides and pilots* who prefer not to hunt in this manner
but are forced into it by competition." Quite apart from their
personal repugnance toward this "spotting and potting" type
of hunting, is the ironical fact that a pilot who flies a party
into camp and later makes a second trip for the pick-up,
actually makes more money than by blooding his aircraft on
a single trip. The former director believes that sportsmen,
should return to the older, leisurely ways of the camp hunt
with its lifelong memories of trophies fairly earned. "It is, or
should be, a game," he declares. "Why not play it square."

Many of the western states have already passed laws
against using airplanes to "drive, herd or pursue game," and
some of them forbid "air to ground signals from pilot to
hunter." Dr. Ira N. Gabrielson, President, Wildlife Management Institute, writes, "I feel sure these laws will be enacted
in every state and country where big game is considered a
valuable resource." In no place are such laws more needed
than in Alaska, and no animal needs them so desperately as
the giant brown bears.

In partially remedial measures to counteract a situation
where ski-equipped airplanes scouted the snow-covered wilds
in the spring to spot-and-pot the big brownies just coming out
of their dens, the latest Alaska regulations have either pro-
hibited spring bear hunting entirely, or waited until most of
the snow had melted before opening the season for a couple of
weeks. But at least one third of the Alaska mainland—that
part lying generally north of the Yukon River—still remains open for ski-plane hunters of grizzlies and polar bears
as studies by the Alaska Department of Fish and Game continue to work toward a solution that will be acceptable to its
very air-minded citizens.

It has the difficult job of promulgating regulations within
its own state constitution, and of enforcing these laws in its

courts. For the wardens there is the tough and dangerous chore of apprehending airborne violators in that tremendous land; the necessity of proving before judge and jury when an aircraft has become an instrument of chase rather than a legitimate way of conveying hunters to or from established or to-be-established camps. This becomes a matter of conscience, of willingness to abide by the rules. In calling on all sportsmen to conform to the golden rule of good conduct, the Boone and Crockett Club is joined by numerous worldwide conservation groups, all crying for an end to abuses by airborne hunters.

One thing sure. As long as a double standard is allowed to exist in Alaska, or anywhere else, the trophy hunter's title to a bear, moose, caribou, and other big-game trophies remains clouded unless he is able to clear it with a special affidavit superseding mere state requirements. It is a strange situation.

¶ Epilogue

Ever since the first breath of life on earth, the smaller forms have had a much better record for holding their own than the outsize animals. Many kinds of mice, shrews, and squirrels are relatively unchanged in thousands of years, while mammoths, sabre-tooths, and other lunkers collapsed by the wayside of adversity. For example, the smaller black bears are still distributed from Arctic Alaska to the Florida Everglades. Likewise, a few medium-sized grizzlies have managed to hang on in four western states and may be able to hide out in the remoter mountains of Canada and Alaska for years to come. But the real bear titans, the half-ton brownies, are already showing the first signs of depletion.

This was undoubtedly a reason why the Alaska Department of Fish and Game named the Alaska Peninsula, Unit 9, for special curbs against airplane hunting. The Peninsula giant bear of this 700-mile stretch of tundra, alder thickets, salmon-filled rivers, and smoking volcanoes is probably the mightiest land carnivore extant, and it has other distinguishing differences from its competing colossus on Kodiak Island. Separated for countless centuries by the stormy waters of Shelikof Strait, the Peninsula giant bear has developed a different shaped head than the Kodiak bear. This was impressed firmly in my mind the day I went trout fishing at False Pass at the tip end of the peninsula.

It had been a sunny-bright August morning. Visibility was so good that I could see for miles across the open tundra to where Shishaldin Volcano's 9,372-foot-high cone poured a wisp of black smoke into the blue of the sky. I thought I could surely spot one of the mammoth brown bears far enough in the distance to avoid contact, so I left my rifle in the dory while I waded upriver a short ways with my fly rod. Schools of red-spotted Dolly Varden trout were splashing among the migrating salmon, and soon my creel sagged full. As I turned to head back to the dory at salt water, I received a shock.

In utter silence a solid bank of fog had crept in from the North Pacific Ocean and was sliding up the river valley toward me like a sinister thing. It had already cut me off from the river mouth and the dory, and suddenly it seemed to wrap around me with its blinding chill. At thirty feet every object appeared fuzzy and alive. In my imagination every clump of alders was a bear. Knowing well how the big bears liked to move around under cover of the fog, I waded out into the center of the stream and started feeling my way down current, floundering and skidding on the backs of the massed salmon. The return seemed to take much longer than the upriver trip, and I wondered if I could possibly be in the wrong channel through the delta. Where the flow narrowed, deepened and turned against a steep clay bank for its final run to salt water, I decided to get out on the shore and follow along its edge to the place I had jammed an oar into the muck and looped the dory painter around it. Before climbing the clay bank I looked up at a blurry dark object ahead, and froze in my tracks, because what I saw was no alder bush.

Staring down on me with deep-set eyes, its great bulk magnified by fog particles until it looked like a woolly elephant out of the ice age, was one of the biggest brown bears I had ever seen in my Alaska travels.

For a moment I was paralyzed at the enormity of the beast. The impact of it robbed me of every muscle and I stood spellbound and truly terrified. All the while the shaggy monster stood posed above me in watchful, soundless appraisal, and I remember how each guard hair glistened with moisture. Its jaws chomped nervously and I caught a glimpse of yellowed teeth the size of my thumbs, and it occurred to me that possibly the great brown bear was as much surprised as I by the sudden encounter.

Then, in that strange way of these giants, the bear turned its head away from me, swung full profile and peered off into the fog as though I didn't exist. In this charged moment— when I knew the beast was watching from the corners of its eyes, waiting for me to make one false move—I noticed that its head was longer and narrower than that of the Kodiak bear, with which I was at that time more familiar. Framed in the fog, it was like the head of an enormous wolf. That was the way I saw it last and always remembered it. As I turned slowly about and sloshed out to my shirt pockets in the deepening river, I stole a final look. The monster hadn't moved. It was still gazing into the mist, pretending not to see me as I faded out of its vision, groped my way to the dory and laid back on the oars.

Through the years I measured many a bear skull with calipers and steel tape to verify this pronounced variation in the shapes of the Peninsula and Kodiak Island brown bears.

An average sized Peninsula bear skull might measure 18 inches long by 11 inches wide. Under the Boone and Crockett Club method for scoring by adding length to width it would register 29. A Kodiak bear of roughly the same body weight might measure 17 inches long by 12 inches wide; an inch shorter, an inch broader, and also registering 29. The Kodiak bear's skull would be more massive in appearance, in fact the most massive of any living predator on earth.

In no way disputing the careful studies of mammalogists who assert that all our brown and grizzly bears are descendants of the European brown bear (*Ursus arctos*) which, as mentioned earlier, spread across Asia to Bering Strait and tramped over a then existing land bridge to Alaska, the American brown bears are of several shapes, sizes, and colors. In addition to the two world champs—the Peninsula giant and the Kodiak bear—there are known to be several more coarsely-haired brownies scattered all the way along the shoreline from Kenai Peninsula east and south to the boundary of British Columbia. Still others are isolated on the A.B.C. Islands (Admiralty, Baranof, Chichagof) in the Tongass National Forest of Southeastern Alaska. Quite aside from the probability that many, if not all, of these bears are not separate species but mere mutations, some of them possess considerable individuality.

One of the oddest bears in America is the Shiras brown bear of Admiralty Island, which is not brown at all, but quite black with coffee-colored underfur. It is found nowhere else in Alaska. Its nearest prototype appears to be a brooding dark giant of the Russian forests. Another massive form is the Dall brown bear reported from glacier-bound Yakutat Bay, though it had a suspicious resemblance to two other named bears on Hinchinbrook and Montague Islands near Cordova in Prince William Sound. All of these bears occasionally produce outsized males rivaling those on Kodiak Island and Alaska Peninsula. And all have one thing in common: Their future is precarious.

Back 75 miles from the Alaska coastline, the Boone and Crockett Club has had to draw an arbitrary line separating, for skull classification, the brown from the grizzly. The sour-tempered Toklat grizzly of the Alaska Range—with its high-shoulder hump; its silky, creamy-white fur rippling in the keen mountain breezes; its long, polished horn-colored claws; its foreshortened skull with its pug-nosed effect—is typical of the group inside this line. Those who believe, and many do, that the biologists have split the descendants of the European brown bear into too many varieties on too meager evidence, might just as well believe that a description of the Toklat grizzly ought to be cut a little roomier. It would then fit other such mountain types as the Kluane grizzly, the Alaska grizzly, the Tanana grizzly, the Tundra bear, and the several other forms found all the way from Montana to the Arctic Ocean.

With no natural barriers keeping them apart, there is much overlapping of range and consequent promiscuous interbreeding between the named kinds of interior grizzlies. When amorous male meets willing female on a warm June morning, nature takes its course. Guide Ralph Young snorts at the hair-splitting "experts" who "discover" new species, and poses this question: "Do the bears go around calipering one another's skulls prior to breeding?"

By whatever names the brown-grizzly variations are called in different regions of Alaska, man's burning desire to shoot the one with the biggest head to gain the plaudits of a Boone and Crockett Club listing emphasizes the need for special protection of the coastal whoppers. In a recent study, the Alaska Department of Fish and Game revealed that Alaska Peninsula headed the recorded annual kill with 121. Kodiak Island was next with 118. The bears from these two areas completely dominated the Boone and Crockett listings, and caused close to 50 percent of all bear hunting to be concentrated on hardly more than 6 percent of the new state!

Against a total take of 402 of all coastal brownies, only 62 grizzly types were shot in all the rest of Alaska. While the Department of Fish and Game felt called upon to issue a statement that in no area were kills excessive, it left no doubt that hunting pressure was by far the heaviest among the giants of Alaska Peninsula and Kodiak Island. It wished trophy seekers would pay more attention to the other half of the country.

A reversal of this concentrated bear shooting has taken place among the polar bear hunters. For countless long winters the Eskimos hunted the great white bear only as it came wandering in from the frozen ocean to their villages along the Arctic coast. The extent of hunting activity, first with spears and later with trading post rifles, was mostly within a narrow perimeter averaging no more than seven or eight miles wide. But in recent years an ominous change, for the bears, has taken place. A combination of small, ski-equipped planes and gutful pilots has pushed the hunting grounds more than 150 miles out over international frozen seas. Circling like falcons over the ice fields, looking down on thousands of square miles, the pilot finds a bear and lands close by. Nanook doesn't have a chance; he is like a cow in a pasture. There is no place to hide. Unless some way is found to trim the wings of these deadly, gas-eating birds through international agreements, curtailments, and enforcement, the polar bear must be considered as a species slated to vanish in the 21st century, possibly sooner in many parts of the Arctic.

Though the white bear has no safety zone except the jumbled ice packs farther and farther from land, closer and closer to the North Pole, the brown-grizzly bears are faring better in the matter of sanctuary. In Alaska, McKinley National Park should continue to house fair numbers of the hump-shouldered mountain grizzlies indefinitely. Glacier Bay National Monument in Southeastern Alaska, a few miles west of Juneau, allows no hunting for its mixed populations of browns, grizzlies, and varicolored blacks. Katmai National Monument, in which are the dying fumaroles of famed Valley of Ten Thousand Smokes, supports a scattering of Peninsula giant bears, and so does Unimak Island Reserve at the east extremity of the Aleutian Islands. Close to a couple of million acres on Kodiak National Wildlife Refuge are being managed to perpetuate the great Kodiak bear. Ability of wildlife groups to fight off special interests in these sanctuaries may determine how long the big bears will survive. An oil strike, a mineral stampede, a defense installation, an army of woodcutters could change things almost overnight.

Under the protective wing of the Alaska Department of Fish and Game is the entire watershed of McNeil River, which flows into Kamishak Bay on lower Cook Inlet southwest of Anchorage. In the summer it is a spectacular showplace of galloping brown bears on the slippery rocks, leaping salmon, roaring rapids, and diving brownies. Along Pack Creek and in the Thayer Mountain Area of Admiralty Island in the Tongass National Forest of Southeastern Alaska, sightseers may observe bears of many shades and sizes swaggering about on their own business, bothering nobody if nobody bothers them. No shooting is permitted by law. Nonetheless, a pall of doom hangs over these Admiralty sanctuaries as it does over every other bear habitat in the park-like beauty of this island. It is caused by the present policy of the U.S. Forest Service of contracting with foreign-owned logging companies to strip the island for pulpwood.

Bear-hunting seasons are similar all through the far north. Alaska, Yukon and Northwest Territories, British Columbia and Alberta Provinces allow hunting in September and October, terminating when the big bears go into hibernation. There is another shooting season in the spring lasting into June. In the lower forty-eight, only Montana and Wyoming still per-

mit grizzly hunting for a few weeks, and this is confined to the
fall. Wyoming adds this significant bit of advice: "Best hunting along borders of Yellowstone Park."

Yet a reasonable number of trophies taken under direction
of local guides is believed to be more beneficial than otherwise.
The removal of surplus stock under the watchful eyes of a
game department is not the real threat to eventual phasing out
of the grizzly clan. If this were the only factor involved, the
big bears might last indefinitely. But the problem is far more
involved.

It is the takeover of entire mountain ranges by domestic
stock to feed more and more people, followed by the demands
of ranchers to destroy cattle-killing bears. It is the scream of
chain saws ripping down primitive forests to feed the pulp
mills. It is the roar of bulldozers gouging off the natural cover
to make room for orchards and gardens for a human population increasing at the fearful rate of 60 million a year in the
world. It is the blasting of dynamite where once was wilderness to pave more miles of highways. What's left for the big
bears isn't much, and it's getting smaller.

By the year 2000, which a dour old-timer dubbed the "Age
of Cement," the only true wilderness will begin in the northern
tips of British Columbia and Alberta, Canada, and extend into
the inhospitable regions of Alaska, Yukon and Northwest
Territories. The smaller, hardier grizzly types with ability to
exist by digging out squirrels and carding wild berries on the
mountain slopes may hang on for as long as there are wild
places to hide from man. But for the huge brown bears of the
humid lower coast, already bypassed by human emigration to
Alaska, there is no comparable reprieve. Industry claims more
of their habitat year by year, and there is no end in sight.

Those bears in the National Forests of Southeastern Alaska,
especially the unique Shiras "black browns" of Admiralty
Island, are being driven from one timbered retreat to another
as logging crews in the employ of Japanese-owned pulp mills

are permitted to bring the big trees crashing down with callous disregard for other assets on this famous island, once proposed by President Teddy Roosevelt as worthy of national recreation status for all the people of America.

How are the bear faring? Not so good, especially on Admiralty Island.

About Frank Dufresne

Most of Frank Dufresne's forty years in and around bear country were spent in Alaska. His early reports were instrumental in helping Congress to frame the first comprehensive Alaska Game Act, and for several years he served as the Director of the Alaska Game Commission.

One of the country's most admired nature writers, Frank Dufresne was an associate editor of *Field & Stream* magazine and a frequent contributor to numerous other publications. He was also well known as the author of *Animals and Fishes of Alaska, The Great Outdoors, Lure of the Open*, and an autobiography, *My Way Was North*.

About Roger Caras, author of the Foreword

Emmy Award-winning Roger Caras is the author of nearly 60 books on animals and wildlife, including a bear book, *Monarch of Deadman Bay*. For nearly twenty years, he has been Special Correspondent for Animals and the Environment for ABC News, the only correspondent ever assigned to that beat exclusively. He lives with his wife and their large collection of animals on a horse farm in Maryland.